ON THE WINGS OF PRAYER

Daily prayers, thoughts and meditations to lift your spirits

By Kathy H. Culmer

EAST 26TH
PUBLISHING

www.east26thpublishing.com

Library of Congress Cataloging-in-Publication data is available

ISBN: Paperback 978-1-955077-90-3 | eBook 978-1-955077-91-0

10 9 8 7 6 5 4 3 2 1
First printing edition 2022

East 26th Publishing
Houston, TX

ON THE WINGS OF PRAYER

Daily prayers, thoughts and meditations to lift your spirits

FORWARD

C. S. Lewis once wrote, "I pray because I can't help myself. I pray because I'm helpless. I pray because the need flows out of me all the time, waking and sleeping. It doesn't change God. It changes me."

The words in this book come up and out of me, though not always so easily. Sometimes by invitation and sometimes without prompting, all on their own, but some time ago I realized they were not for me alone. More than ten years ago (2012), I was prompted to begin these writings after reading a Facebook post about someone who wrote daily prayers. My chance reading of this post challenged me to write a daily prayer and share it with *my* Facebook friends. My attempt was originally made as a challenge more to myself than anything else, but when friends began to respond with their likes and comments, I began to see the prayers as more of an offering, more as an opportunity to plant a seed of positivity into the lives of others.

Some days the words would come to me as prayers, some days as an extended thought, and some days as longer reflections. All of these, over time, have resulted in this collection. Not long ago, a reader and follower of my postings wrote, "Thank you so much for sharing your beautiful thoughts/prayers/meditations. They bless my days." Whether the words found within these pages provide the reader with moments of quiet reflection, supply you with just the right words when you don't know what to pray, or just add a smile to your day, my prayer is that they will bless your days and lift your spirits in unexpected ways.

In the book of Jeremiah, we find this passage, "When I discovered your words, I feasted on them; and they became my joy, the delight of my heart." (Jeremiah 15:16)

 It would certainly be my delight if you will find something among these words to feast upon and bring you joy.

Blessings!
Kathy

1

My Heart: God's Dwelling Place.

O God, you stitched me together with precision and to perfection
in my mother's womb even after You first gave thought to me.

You watched over me while I was being formed and taking shape.

You knew when I would draw my first breath.
You gave it to me.
You will be there to catch my last.

You knew I would come to this moment, this time, this place,
(like every other moment I have come to) and You prepared me for it
beforehand.

I am always living into the plan that was laid before me.
There is nothing about me that surprises You!

You equipped me,
Lacking nothing,
But with space,
Space enough to grow,
And space to be filled,
Space that could only be filled by You.

So that as my heart longed for and opened itself up,
You would come in and be seated upon its throne,
Making it Your home and forever dwelling place.

I was designed with this plan and purpose in mind.

My Designer is a Perfectionist!

A Visionary, A Perfectionist, A Mastermind My Designer is!

2

Because of Your great love, O God, we are not consumed.

We are not overtaken.

Though winded, we do not faint.

Though bent, we are not broken.

Though despised, we are not unloved.

And if we fall—no when we fall—because surely there will be a when, we do not stay fallen.

Through You and in You and with You, we are raised up—to our knees, to our feet, to our standing once more.

Whatever the depth to which we descend, O God, Your hand of mercy to us You extend.

To lift us up again.

With thanksgiving we look back and we look up and we look forward and say

But, for You, O God!

Thank You! Thank You! Thank You! and Amen!

Kathy Culmer

3

What if every time we thought it was going to rain,
we refused to go outside?

What if every time we saw a storm cloud,
we went looking for a place to hide?

If nothing else, we'd never get to see a rainbow or a silver lining if all we did was stay hidden—sheltered inside while waiting for the storm cloud to pass or the rain to subside.

What joy, what beauty, what other such reward, for fear's sake, have we been denied for never having tried or having dared to go outside?

4

The darkest part of night comes just before it ends.

After the bleakness of winter, we see all around
New growth that the earth sends.

During childbirth, the hardest push and the greatest pain come
Just before new life begins.

When it looks as though the storm will never end,
The sun comes shining through and calms its winds.

The darkness, the pain, the bleakness, the rain
are not there to break you.

They are, instead, your break through
breaking through.

At the appointed time,
what has already been accomplished on your behalf,

Will be made known to you.
And your long-awaited breakthrough will break through for you.

Kathy Culmer

5

*"We should go up and take possession of the land,
for we can certainly do it."*
Num. 13:30

Fear and doubt see the giant as a thing that can't be beat, and so they seek retreat.

"The giant is too big," they say and run away.

But Faith sees God when some giant we meet.
It knows that with God's help, the giant will suffer defeat.
The eyes of faith will see and show that the giant is a conquerable foe.

Giants may look daunting but are rarely as unconquerable as they appear to be.

They just seem that way when we only trust in what we can see.
In the face of Faith the giant must flee or risk destruction or captivity.
Faith trusts the unseen and is confident that the Trusted One will give us victory.

When the giant stands in our way, O God, help us to see and put our trust in You, our giants to slay.

Strengthen us to take a stand, go in and take possession of our promised land, anyway. Thank You and Amen.

6

O God, whose dawn has never once been late,
whose tides know exactly when to swim in and out again,
whose earth by Your command on its axis spins,

A new day to create
to begin on time
all the time
every day
again and again.

O God, who is both timeless and timely ,
who will be with me, without fail, until life in this world comes to an
end and on and on throughout eternity, world without end.

O God, You Are—now and then—in time and out of time.
Will ever be, and always have been!

Thank You and Amen.

7

"He makes my feet like the feet of deer and sets me on my high places."
Psalm 18:33 (NKJV)

Mountain climbing is not an easy thing to do. A mere rock beneath our feet can be uncomfortable and can cause unsteadiness, and we would most certainly be overwhelmed by the thought of treading upon a gargantuan rock.

Our feet were not made for climbing big rocks. Not without a covering anyway. They were not made for scaling mountains, without help from another source. The heights are too great, the terrain too rugged, the conditions unbearable at certain altitudes, and the risk of falling, too threatening.

Most of us will never climb an actual mountain, but we will certainly be faced with many mountains throughout the journey of our lives.

There will be obstacles that seem mountain-like—insurmountable, unclimbable.

There will be summits that seem unreachable.
The heights will simply seem too great.
The climb too difficult.
Our footing too unsure.

But, the promise of the One who inspired the Psalmist is that,

"He makes my feet like the feet of deer, and sets me on my high places."
Psalms 18:33 (NIV)

He will make me to run where I could not even walk.
He will make me to glide past the impassable.
He will give to me new feet to scale the heights for which I was not made in the flesh to climb, but to which I ever aspire.

He will give me all that I need to make the climb and to make it without falling and without fail.

It is no accident that the mountain is there, for it, too, is part of God's creation.

His plan.
His Divine purpose.

It is not there to defeat us or even to make us turn back.

The mountain is not there to hinder, but to remind us of our dependence on a power greater than ourselves, to remind us of the vastness of our world, and, ultimately, to take us to greater heights.

Though the terrain is rugged and the climb steep, God will make our footing sure, until our journey is complete.

We must believe His promise, and we must trust Him to give us feet to climb. It is through such trusting and believing that we will reach our "high places." Places that will allow us to see clearer and farther. Places where we were purposed to be.

God alone can set us upon those heights, and with each one reached, He takes us higher and higher and draws us closer and closer to Himself.

8

*"For I am the Lord your God Who holds your right hand,
and Who says to you, 'Do not be afraid I will help you.'"*
Isaiah 41:13

Carrying Heavy Loads

When it seems that our load is too heavy, we wonder why.

Sometimes the load we carry is too heavy because, well, simply because we are carrying too much of a load.

Sometimes it is too heavy because we try to carry our load alone.

Other times the load we carry appears to be too heavy because of how we look at it or how we perceive the load we are carrying.

Sometimes we are given a heavy load to carry in order to increase our endurance and expand our capacity for weight lifting, and so that we can help others who cannot carry theirs alone.

And sometimes, our load is heavy because we are the most abled ones to carry the weight of it.

Thank You, O God, that no matter the load we carry, we do not carry it alone.

Amen.

9

When adversarial winds blow
and our boughs from the stress of their force are bent low

When there are storm clouds above and
rough waters below

With much of our journey yet to go

With Christ our companion

This for certain we know

Such winds when they blow
necessarily so

Come not to consume
But to strengthen and lengthen our roots down below.

And our faith so that it, and we, may strengthen and grow.

Kathy Culmer

10

If you feel that you've been going through,

that times are tough and you don't know how you're going to make it or know what to do,

I say to you, keep going!

Don't stop.

Through is not a place to stop and stay, but a place of pause as you go on your way.

Through may be for you—

The desert sand that you must cross to get to your promised land,

The wilderness where you must abide until some door is open and you can go inside,

The valley where you must temporarily stop on the way to your next mountain top,

Or, your journey through may be like a tumultuous sea whose waters must part to open the way for you to go through.

Whatever through is for you,
Keep going.

Until your going through has brought you through.

Led you back into the light and set you upon the height.

Kathy Culmer

11

When Silence Speaks

Sometimes the silence can say more than we want to hear.

Could that be why we have so much fear of the silence?

Sometimes we keep talking and let words get in the way, just to keep from hearing what the silence has to say.

Some things, however, only the silence can teach us or tell us, or provide for us.

So putting our fears and discomfort aside, we must let silence speak, have its say and listen to it, whether or not we want to, anyway.

12

Going Through

Sometimes you just have to go through stuff!

Sometimes you have to go through just to get through what you have to get through.

Sometimes you go through to know how to go through
or that you can go through when you have to.

Sometimes you go through so you can know how you got through,
so you can help somebody else through or show them how to go
through or convince them that they can get through too.

Sometimes going around, another way or avoiding what's in front of you
all together just won't do.

You just have to go through!

But, the One who has made us and who enables us says, "Fear not!
When you pass through whatever you're going through, I will be with
you…" (Isaiah 43:2)

13

You are, O God

O God, you are the Lover of my soul

The Healer of my woe

You are the Shepherd who leads me in the way I should go, then leads me back to the way when I stray

You are the strength that I need when I can't find my own

The One who refreshes me when my strength is all gone

You are the Company I keep,
or that keeps me

when I feel all alone

My pain and my sorrow, right beside me You feel

There's no ache in my body, or heart, that You cannot heal

My Shield and Defender, You won't let me fall prey

You are the Restorer of all that the locust-predator-enemy has taken away

Jehovah-Shalom, in You, our peace we will find

You speak to our storms and chase them away
saying, "Peace. Be still."

Your voice they obey

What once raged about or within us,
at Your command,

Kathy Culmer

becomes tranquil.

You are

PeaceJoyLoveTeacherComforterSaviorLordFriend

and so much more

The answer to our every need

You say Your name is, "I AM."

With   gratitude and humility, I say,
You are All indeed!

Thank You and Amen!

14

When your dream refuses to come true
Gets crushed, or seems a bit nightmarish to you
And you just don't know what else to do

Cry, but do not let your tears blind you.
Grieve, but do not let your grief bind you.
Be angry, but do not let bitterness cover you or consume you or linger
too long
So that reason cannot find you.

Be disappointed, but do not let disappointment hinder you, but incline
you
To act with bold intention and without apprehension.
Let all you face and fear and dread not suppress you but remind you
There is still work to do. Much work to do.
Do, but don't grow weary in your doing!

There's a power far greater than yourself that's assigned you
Moving in you
Before you
Beside you
And behind you
For dream-making and making dreams come true.

So, stand boldly on your faith and let nothing undermine you.

15

"They are like trees planted along a riverbank, with roots that reach deep into the water. Such trees are not bothered by the heat or worried by long months of drought. Their leaves stay green, and they never stop producing fruit."

Jer. 17:8 (NLT)

Like a Tree…
The sturdiest tree does not grow in the shade
Under the covering of sky alone, but out in open air it is made.

Its roots watered by adversity,
Grow wide and deep in the earth where only God can see.
Its trunk thickened to be a means of defense,
Toughened to stand by battling the elements.

Its branches battered by storm winds
That have caused them to stoop low under the weight
Forced them to bow under pressure though never break
Winds they breathed in and out as fresh air
Winds that lengthened and strengthened them so
They could outward go and upward grow.
Till the tree could stand at its full height,
Make its own shade and provide cover and shelter for which it was made.

To You, O God, who makes us and makes us to grow, may we, "A planting of the Lord for the display of Your splendor," remain always rooted and grounded in You. May our roots grow deep, our cores grow sturdy and strong, our branches long--far-reaching and wide. Though sometimes shakable, may we remain always unbreakable. And may we bear fruit that is sweet to Your taste and nurturing to the body.

Amen.

Kathy Culmer

16

Every time I open my eyes
I've been given a chance to realize
Anew
That I've made it out of darkness and once more come through.

That my darkness was a temporary stay
Until my eyes would be opened to the light of a new day.

Every hardship that we've hoped to avoid and tried to pray away, and
that You, allowed anyway.

By your grace and goodness, Lord, we have made it through.

Maybe that's what going through is supposed to do—

Show us that we can,
Yes, we can,
When we trust in You.

Rest in peace and wake up anew.

Amen.

17

Facing the Storm

We cannot know what storms await us,
What tumultuous winds will blow to agitate us,
What crushing waves will rise to devastate us!

When they'll come,
How long they'll last,
How fiery their blast.

But come they will.

So, it behooves us to know
The One who commands the winds and waves so

Telling them to come or go
The Master of sky and sea and earth below
Who by His Word can redirect the storm and tell its winds where they
may blow.

Or by His will
Calm the winds and make the storm be still.

Grant us peace, O Lord, and keep us safe until
the storm has passed.

Amen.

18

I wonder as I wander

When you think out loud, can anyone hear you?
When you walk in the dark, can you see what you do?
The other day, I got up before sound
The light of day was yet to be found
Critters weren't even stirring or moving around.
Walking along in the dark, I started thinking out loud about the new day,
And found my thoughts had a lot to say.

How do birds know when to begin their song,
When they've been sleeping all night long?
How do the squirrels know when to start their daily fun run?
How does the sun know when time comes for it to show?
Or the wind know when and which way to blow?
How does any of creation know?
Must be that the Creator made and told them so.

Kathy Culmer

19

*"Still other seeds fell on fertile soil, and they produced a crop that was
thirty, sixty, and even a hundred times as much as had been planted!"*
Mt. 13:9

When birds scatter seed they don't know
Where the seed will take root down below
Some seed will die, some will grow.
The bird doesn't know. It just lets go.

What would it be like if more of us lived so?
Stopped holding and withholding and just let go?

What difference it would make!
What lives would be changed!

Unless we do,
We will never know.

Help me, O God, to live as generously,
Spreading seeds of kindness and goodness wherever I can or might be,
Not worrying about whether it'll be received, or how, or if it will come
back to me.
Just living and giving and loving free.
Being a model of Your love for others to see.

Kathy Culmer

20

Blessed God who has set us in our course and equipped us for it.

Who has foreseen the landscape of our lives, prepares us for it and travels it with us.

We give You thanks for feet to scale the heights.
For strength and the will to climb.
For periods of rest and recovery and discovery in the in-between-time.

We thank You for feet that are adaptable and suitable to walk the plain.
That enable us to navigate whatever the terrain.

And when our own feet falter, that You carry us until we can stand on our own again.

Thank You and Amen.

21

Once Upon a Day Out Walking

In the midst of the cloud-filled sky, I observed a patch of blue
A wink from my Boo, saying, "I've got my eye on you."

In the discomfort of the day's heat, I felt a cool breeze
Ahhhhhhh

My Main Squeeze, blowing me a kiss across the top of the trees.

In the midst of the quiet, I was just walking along
When I heard the bird's tweet.
A melody sweet, but oh so strong.
My Beloved's voice singing me a love song!

Then, I heard my Beloved say,
Clear as day
(In my head anyway)
By chance,
Do you wanna dance?

Love notes here and there
Reminders to keep me well aware,
That the Lover of my Soul is always there
With and around me everywhere.

As you read these words
May you find in them grace,
To see in them your Beloved's face,
And feel Love's warm embrace.

Kathy Culmer

22

"I have loved you with an everlasting love."
Jeremiah 31:3

Loved us.
Loves us still.
Yesterday.
Today.
And until.
And no matter what,
Always will!
Amen.

23

The Lord is my Shepherd,
Though I sometimes forget.
All my needs have been, will be, and are even now, being met.
Even where I have not seen the manifestation yet.

Fulfillment will come
in time—
an appointed time—
a time already set.

Yes, because the Lord is my Shepherd.

The Great Shepherd,
The Good Shepherd,
The Shepherd who has never lost one of his sheep.

His life laid down in wretched sleep.

My soul, my life, my all to keep.

I need not worry, doubt or fret!
Ever!

Thank You and Amen!

Kathy Culmer

24

A new day!
To be kissed by the sun and
Blessed by the Son.
What a glorious way to begin it!
Savor every minute.
Hold fast the life in it.
Though you may wish to hurry past,
Make each breath last.
Soon enough,
Without your worry or your hurry,
It will have all passed.
Too fast.

Kathy Culmer

25

Adversity comes to not only show us our true selves, but to help us become our best selves.

26

Perhaps I'll see something that I didn't see yesterday
or see it differently
if need be.

That's the gift and the challenge of a new day.
You get to do what you've done before once more
or something new
or the old in a new way if you want to.

Most times it's up to you.

Kathy Culmer

27

Prayer.
Sometimes prayer is the way to the answer.
Sometimes prayer is the key that is turned to release the answer.
Sometimes it is the lock that is opened to receive the answer.
Sometimes it is our awe and offering in response to the answer.
But no matter what, in all things and always, prayer is the answer.

28

And there was evening and there was morning, another day,
Out of darkness, God called the light, and thus each new day begins in
the middle of the night.

Night does not take its rest in darkness, though its work we cannot see.

It is moving, moment by moment, steadily.

Back towards the light it will reach eventually, so that once more by its
light we can see.

Even in darkness, work is being done that we can't glean, though done
on our behalf, it remains unseen. Night does its work in darkness, and
there does it best, while we sleep and from our worry rest.

In the course of our every day, we must experience darkness before we
see light. Day even begins in the middle of the night, while the new day
is making its way to the light.

Even the earth does not sleep all at the once. While we, on one side of
the earth, walk in light, the other side is experiencing night.

It was even out of darkness that in the beginning, God gave the
command to bring forth the light.

Though we must go through darkness necessarily, it is to be with us
only temporarily. After the work of the night, comes the return of the
light.

Though from time to time, we must walk in darkness, O God, we thank
You for Your abiding light. Whenever it is necessary for us to go there,

we pray that You will guide us and guard us and sustain us with Your loving care, until our night has ended and light returns again.

Thank You and Amen!

29

The sun sets, not so that it can take its rest,
but so that we can.
Or will.
If we will.

The sun rises, not to wake itself up from the night,
but so that we can see .
In a new light.
Or will.
If we will.

30

Growing Toward the Light

Before a seed can become what it was meant to be, it must be planted in the earth below.

There, under the cover of darkness it can grow.

When the darkness has held it long enough, upward it will go,
through the perils of darkness it will reach for the light,
stretching upward towards the sun,
until it reaches some new height.

Like the seed, in order to become what we were meant to be and live more fully into our possibility, at times, the darkness we too must undergo. So that we can upwards grow, ever reaching for the Son.

Growing toward the light.

31

The Sky is Still Blue

You know how you can sometimes, at just the right moment,
look up into a cloud covered-sky
when something catches your eye.
You've been walking around feeling dismal with your eyes and your
spirit cast down, when suddenly your focus is shifted and you're
prompted to lift your head and fix your gaze up high

And when you do, you see a patch of blue peeking through,
looking like it's looking right at you,
to gladden your heart or your hope renew?

Yeah, that's what looking up can do for you,
or looking through cloud-cover to discover a patch of blue.

Though for a while that bright spot has been out of view,
it appears at just the right time to remind you that storms don't always
last,
that underneath the clouds the sky is still blue, and that it's just a matter
of time before the sun breaks through.

Just because the clouds in the sky are gray, it doesn't mean that the blue
sky is gone away.

At least not to stay.

It is just waiting its turn to once more show itself blue and the sun to
reveal itself (in the unlikeliest of ways) and come shining through.

The Creator of all who still holds the earth and sky and all of creation in
His hands is working unseen to carry out his plans.

Amen.

Kathy Culmer

32

Wonder what God's voice sounded like in the beginning when He called creation to be?

Was it the sound of a whisper, a gentle breeze or the howling sea?

Was it with a roar that God called out of nothingness that which never was before?

Was it with the sound of "peace be still" that creation obeyed and made manifest the Creator's will?

Was it with the sound of a thought that the Creator made the call, bidding things to come forth with words not heard at all?

Did God's voice sound like silence or perhaps a symphony, when it called out over the vastness of eternity, over that which never before had been and said, "Let there be, "

33

A Reminder:

And I will set my bow in the clouds,
and it shall be a reminder to you that

 God's got this!

34

Worldview

The world is so much bigger than me.
There's so much more that I can see
When I take my eyes off me.

When I take my eyes off me,
There's so much more of the world that I can see.

If I would dare to look beyond perceived possibility.

The world is sooooo much bigger than you and me!
But I have to cast my vision past myself to see.

When I open my eyes wide,
Truths that have been hidden can no longer hide.
Nor the hope of what can be.
If I in the other,
Regardless of proximity,
Would dare to see myself in them and them in me.

How much better together are we
When we can ourselves see
One in the other and the other in me.

As You, O God, made us from the beginning to be.

Kathy Culmer

35

While you cannot resist God enough to keep God from reaching out to touch you, you can resist God enough so that you don't feel God's touch when He does.

O God, let us not go untouched.! Help us to resist every inclination to do so. No matter how far out of touch we may be, never let us get so far we are beyond reaching.

And help us, O God, to miss no opportunity to reach out to touch others, resisting every inclination not to do so with Your love.

Amen.

Kathy Culmer

36

Sometimes when I'm sitting and talking with my husband, (not calling any names), I get annoyed because he seems to be distracted.

He is either looking at his phone or tv or the computer.

(Truth be told, I do the same things sometimes, but that's not the point)

I get annoyed and feel slighted because I want his full attention.

He is sometimes quick to say, "But I'm right here with you."

And he is, to an extent, but not fully.

And while I enjoy occupying the same space at the same time with him and appreciate his near proximity, our time together is so much more enjoyable, so much more meaningful, so much richer when we are both fully present and our attention is focused on one another, whether or not we exchange words.

I wonder if that is at all how God feels about us and the time we spend with Him in prayer.

37

The heavens declare

Perhaps it is not by chance that we must look upward to get a glance of both the sun and the Son,
that we must look up to see,
though because of their brightness, never fully seeing.

Perhaps it is not incidental that each is a source of light and life,
that each resides in the heavens and reigns on earth,
that their position and the need for their provision require us to look upward,
and that a deficit of either's light can result in our experiencing S.A.D.ness,

Seasonal Affective Disorder brought on by the lack of sun/Son-light.

Could it then be so, that by Divine design living things need both sun and Son light to live and grow,
to draw us in the direction we ought to go and to keep us looking upward as a reminder to do so.

38

In my bed as I lay drifting into consciousness,
I heard a whisper say,

Welcome, Beloved, you get to live another day!

Do your part and make the best of it,
I'll take care of the rest of it.
Live in joyful expectation
the whole day through
and you will find hidden treasures placed just for you.

When you come to those hard places—
.and you may—
don't let them take your joy away.

Treasure every minute and may you find the grace that's in it.
Enjoy life with all its highs and lows too
and, if you can, help somebody else to!

Keep your eyes and heart on me throughout the day.
I've got your back in every way.
As I've touched you, go touch somebody else today.

Love. Abba. With a kiss!

Kathy Culmer

39

Sometimes,
especially when feeling breathless or holding our breath too long for fear
of letting go or that it will not return,
We must
Let go
and let God
Let go
and b--r--e--a--t--h--e--
and let God catch the breath
and us!

40

Stop Lights

I did it. I walked past the traffic light that had for so long been the turnaround point during my morning walk.

That light had been my signal to stop, turn around and go back home.

Never before had it even occurred to me that I could or should walk past the light to go any further.

It was the self-imposed stopping point I had determined years before.

Traffic lights are put in place to moderate traffic flow and to facilitate safety. They warn us to slow down and then to stop so that others can have a turn, so that we don't all try and go at the same time and risk colliding.

Sometimes they may give you a place to catch your breath.
But by no means does every stop light we come to in life mean we need to stop, turn around and go home.

Sometimes the stop light can simply be a place for us to rest until the traffic clears.

41

"For he satisfies the thirsty soul and fills the hungry soul with good"
Psalm 107:9 TLB

O Eternal One...
Whose presence reaches across the heavens
and from shore to shore
Who at creation called out of nothingness
that which never was before
Who shaped humanity into being
up from earth's floor
To be Your crowning glory!
Whose love has covered us since time before
And will until forevermore!

O Eternal One whom I adore,
Fall fresh upon me
Revive
Renew
Restore
Filling me anew once more
With Your Spirit through and through
So that I myself may fully be
And You may Be all the more in me.

42

Some of us don't like to stretch.
Stretching moves us from the comfortable
and the used-to
to the unfamiliar and the new.

We fear it will cause us some unnecessary pain or leave us feeling sore
from the excess strain.

Even when we have a regular workout routine, we may skip the
stretching because its results cannot immediately be seen.

Stretching increases our flexibility, protects our joints and expands our
reach.

In some cases, it can result in clarity and tranquility when willing to let
our inhibitions go free.

Try something new just to see.

Besides,
how could we
reach shelves too high or take a bite of that pie in the sky?
How could we
better know or more fully grow?

What butterflies or dreams would we ever catch
Unless we are willing to reach out and stretch?

Kathy Culmer

43

Hold on to life and don't let go.

Hold on to God so you won't have to.

Kathy Culmer

44

We cannot know that the last time is the last until it has passed.

We cannot calculate the middle unless we know where the thing begins and ends.

Time is precious and priceless.

We pay by the minute with the life we put in it.

We count the cost,
not by how much—
that we can't tell—
but how well
we spend it before it is all spent.

We cannot borrow or lend time, only spend it.

There is no way to refund, repay or rescind it.

Kathy Culmer

45

Made in Your image,
growing into the likeness of You,
showing forth Your glory when I am open and willing,
or opened,
to let Your Will in,
so You can show through.

You know, O Lord, how far I've come,
where I am,
and where I've yet to go.

How and how much I need to grow,
where to expand and detract me so that Your image, Your likeness, Your
glory, can show.

For the daily crafting You do,
Your hands and Your love always upon me,
shaping me into the me that's most pleasing to You.

Thank You and Amen!

46

"Do not let your anger cause you to sin."
Ephesians 4:26

Anger, when left unattended,
Becomes a bitter root that produces fruit
Bitter to taste
and such a waste.
Non-consumable,
Yet all-consuming.
If you let it take hold,
It will take control and keep eating away at your soul.
Do not give in
to anger.
Do not buy into the notion that if you keep holding onto it,
You somehow win,
Or that you're somehow a loser because you give in.
Those are lies.
There is no winner and no prize.

47

Until the Cake is Done

My mother was a good baker, especially of pound cakes. Although I never learned to bake like my mother, I did learn a few lessons from her baking. After she'd stirred up the cake, as she would say, she would pour it into a pan and place it into a pre-heated oven set on the suggested temperature, then she would go about the rest of her chores while it baked. Although she left it in the oven to cook, she would check on it from time to time. Even so, she refused to open the oven door until the cake was done (or nearly done, at the earliest). Instead, she would turn on the oven light and watch it rise through the oven window. She insisted that opening and shutting the door could hinder the cake's rising and make it fall. So with the certainty that the cake would turn out as desired/intended, she would check it periodically to watch its progress, taking care to not hinder its rising.

When I think of Paul's words about prayer, "Pray without ceasing..." I thought of my mother and her cake-baking and cake-watching. After doing what she knew to do with the ingredients to bake the best cake, she put it all in the oven where the baking takes place, checking on it, but trying not to hinder it from rising—trusting the oven to do its job.

Pray without ceasing. Even when we are given an estimated baking time, there are variables determined by the oven you are using that will affect the actual cooking time; that will determine when its done and ready to eat. Pray and don't stop. Keep checking on your cake. Peek and keep on peeking through the oven door. Watch and wait with the expectation that your cake will rise and that it will turn out just right.

48

"In returning to me and resting in me will you be saved.
In quietness and confidence is your strength."
Isaiah 30:15

Listening to the Quiet

When you listen to the quiet
Do you take the time
Are you so inclined?
And when you do,
should you,
What do you hear?
Whispers in the wind, a voice from within or something that has
nothing to do with sound at all,
Deep to deep's call?
How is what you hear heard
By voice or some unspoken word?
When you listen to the quiet
What does it have to say?
Does it comfort, cajole or clarify in any way?
Or do you ignore it and get on with your day, avoid it altogether,
supposing it has nothing or nothing worthwhile to say?
Isn't that what quiet time is anyway_
A time that goes without saying?

Kathy Culmer

49

Misery's goal is to gather all the companions it can find.
Let misery's companionship not be yours and mine.

They say, "Misery loves company."
Just don't let that be you and me.

Negativity's goal is to rob us blind.
It will keep us from all the love, joy and peace of mind, we might otherwise find or ever hope to get.

Help us, Lord, to make sure that goal is not met.

They can be users, too, if that's what we let them do.
After they've robbed us of our joy, they'll use us to rob somebody else's too, if that's what we let them do.

But, we don't have to.

Please don't let us let them.

Misery and its offspring, Negativity, will do all they can to entice you and me.

Help us their schemes to see and recognize, so we won't buy into their lies.

Let us, instead, embrace positivity, that clears our vision and lets us a brighter day see, with all its beauty and possibility.

Help us, O God, not to focus on those things that distort and obstruct our view, that hinder our growth and our walk with You. Help us to discern what is good and true and to that live according to.

Thank you and Amen!

50

In the Shelter of God's Arms

Who is it that bids us to, "Come," when we are weary and coming
undone
Who gives ease to our burdens, making them light
Puts wind beneath our wings to give us our flight

Upon whose shoulders do we stand
And together with them, in whose hand
For even they who came before us and before us have gone
Making a way, the way, their way, did not do so alone
Neither they nor we had strength/legs to stand on our own

Who is it that bids us, "Come"
And see
And taste
And be
Rest and not be weary
Joy more completely
Live, not just merely
But more abundantly
Not just here and now, but eternally
Should we come

Who is it that bids us, "Come,"
And with open arms will gladly receive
Again and again
All who heart-full-y come and in Him believe

That I might come and come again to You, O God, and find welcome,
And that when I cannot do so on my own, You come for me

Thank You and Amen.

Kathy Culmer

51

That mountain that's looming large in front of you
Used to be a rock, until it grew.
Then it became a hill that continued to grow and build
Until it became an obstacle too big for you.
That thing that was once small enough to fit in your hand
Went on to expand
Until it could no longer fit yours, but required a much larger Hand.

Even so, Lord, our mountain is but a rock to You
A thing that can easily fit in Your mighty Hand
And be disassembled at Your command!

Help us, O Lord, .in the face of our mountains to know and do what is
necessary to go over, go around, or to go through.

Thank You that for every mountain that we come to,
You stand ready,
For our asking,
To help us climb over or see us through,
Giving us sturdier legs while You do,
And bringing us up higher, closer and nearer to You!

Thank You and Amen!

52

What if the waters surrounding you —

The waters that you feared would sweep you away,
that appeared to be too wide and too deep to navigate on your own,
that you were certain were there to drown you were actually waters of
baptism?

What if your free fall (or what feels like one) is really an altar call?

What if the above-your-head waters in which you find yourself are there
not to consume you, but are there to purify, to cleanse, heal, and
empower you?

What if that which first took your breath away and even kept it for a
while, that slammed against you and tossed you about (causing you to
doubt) did not come to defeat you but to teach you how to swim?

What if the rough and rugged waters that you dreaded (yet somehow
treaded anyway) would take your life away indeed came to give you
new life?

How does how you see affect your sea?

53

Life Can Be Hard
Life can be hard and tough times will come.

If we are not careful and prayerful,
We can come undone.

But don't.

What looks hopeless only appears that way.
It is a temporary condition; it is not meant to stay.

Uninvited and unwelcome,
Such times may
Too long stay.

So it may feel
Or so you may say.

But, do not dismay.
Keep the faith.
And let it keep you.

Believe.
Pray.
Time and its Author
In time
Will return
And restore
And perhaps even more
All that appeared to have been taken away.

Kathy Culmer

54

Beauty is about so much more than we can see.
 The eyes cannot tell the whole story, just part.

You are a work of art!
Rendered by your Creator's own heart,
not yet finished but already complete,
still becoming what you can't yet see,
all God planned and purposed you to be.

Even the mistakes and the messes
that you make from time to time,
 God's already worked them into your design.

You are made in the image of the Divine.
whose engraving upon your life says,
"You are my beloved, and you are mine."

You are a masterpiece in the making,
without a doubt, from the inside out!

Kathy Culmer

55

While out walking, I approached two buzzards, those disgusting creatures that prey on dead things. One was in the grass just off from the sidewalk, plucking at some dead animal, squirrel, possum or other poor creature that had lost its life in the fight, while the other one was positioned dead center on the sidewalk where I had to pass. Now, these were some big buzzards, cause I guess they've got lots of dead stuff to feed on.

Since I don't know whether buzzards are attack animals or not, and I didn't have time to Google it, I was a little nervous as I approached, and wondering what to do, I just started yelling at them to get out of the way.

To my surprise, they started to walk or hop, or however it is they move, slowly out of the way over towards the wooded area to the left of the sidewalk. In response to my voice/command, they started to move out of the way, although they didn't get in any kind of hurry, or attempt to fly or otherwise react quickly. They just slowly moved into the brush and waited there until I was out of sight so they could resume feasting on their prey.

Sin and temptation, that's how they work. They don't fly away when discovered or even go that far away. They just sit waiting somewhere out of sight, waiting for the interruption to pass so they can resume picking and plucking and gnawing at whatever they are seeking to devour.

Oh yeah. When I was walking back, heading towards home, the buzzards were back at it. This time, there were two young ladies approaching from the opposite direction. As they came closer, the buzzards flew up into the tree whose branches reached out across the sidewalk and waited on a couple of tree branches for them to pass by. They didn't bother to fly away from me. I can only guess that they saw the two as a greater threat than me alone. Indeed, when walking with a trusted companion, we stand a greater chance of upsetting the enemy's plan than when walking alone.

56

To get to the sweetness of the fruit, you have to go past the peeling.

Life can be a lot like that.

To get to the sweetest part, we have to get past the feeling.

For the storms that bowed me, but didn't break me;
For tumultuous times that tossed me about, but didn't take me;
For trials that battered, bruised and sometimes dragged me down, but couldn't shake me;
For the painful truths I had to learn, so they could wake me;
For the hands that used it all to mold and shape and make me.

Through it all, never once, O God, did You leave me or forsake me!

Thank You and Amen.

57

I Wonder as I Wander
How does the river know which way to flow
Or the wind when and which way to blow?
How do the flowers and the green grass know
When to wake from their wintry nap and once more grow?
How does the sun know when to shine and when to hide its glow?
How do the seasons know when to come and when to go,
Or the waters above the earth when to fall as rain, when as snow?
How do the mountains know how high to reach?
And the valleys how low?
The birds to make their home in the wide open air ?
And the four-legged creatures on the earth below?
How does the hare know to make haste and the tortoise to move so
slow (and still win the race)?
How does breath know when it has run its earthly course?
And the time comes to return to its source?
On their own they cannot know, when and where and how to go
But trust, they must, their Maker,
As must we ,
To make the way and guide them so.
To make the way and guide them in the way to go.

Kathy Culmer

58

Guilt and Shame will choke the life out of you.
If you let them.

With their crooked fingers wrapped about your neck, they will hold your promise by the throat.
Their choke hold will cause you to stumble and sway,
lose your consciousness and your way.

Guilt and Shame will clog your pores with their lies,
cause you to shun others and your own self despise.
Their grip will constrict your airwaves and stunt your growth.
They will cut off your lifeline to others convincing you it's your fault they didn't stay
or convincing you you are better off 'cause they were fake any way.
Guilt and Shame will squeeze and squeeze until they take the breath right out of you.
If you let them.

That's what they intended from the beginning to do—
Cut you off from the life that was purposed and planned for you.
When you give Guilt and Shame your power and let them have their way,
Your will becomes their easy prey, and you the slave of what they say.
They will get in your head and try to stay, because that's the control station for what you do and say.

Guilt and Shame will hold your tongue so truth can't have its say and get in their destructive way.
Self-destruction is the ultimate prize for Guilt and Shame in the game they so masterfully play.
They want to hold your truth in captivity.
Truth, they know, will set you free.
Knowing and living your own truth will defeat Guilt and Shame and give you victory.

Kathy Culmer

59

What if God sang creation into being?
Music makes folks move when they hear the sound.
When they hear that trill,
They just can't keep still.
Or that syncopated sound
That can whirl them all around.

They can't help it when they hear the beat.
When two notes meet,
(Don't let the notes repeat)
It will either get them out of their seat
Or make them pat their feet.
Music stirs things up and moves them about.
I wonder if God's breath danced on the waters when He at creation
started calling things out?

What was the rhythm of creation, did God say or sing the sound?
If so, did God sing it pianissimo or let it resound?
What if God sang the world into being and didn't just say the words?
I wonder if the song of creation is the one God gave the birds?
Or if God's, "Let it be," had a melody?
I wonder if the sun and moon were hung with a tune?

Maybe that's why
When people cannot otherwise get around,
When age or sickness has the body and/or mind bound,
When people can no longer do or say,
Or respond in any other way,
If you turn on the music or put on an old familiar tune and let it play,
In time, they will start to bob or snap or from side-to-side sway,
Cause music moves stuff and moves in us that way.

If God sang creation into being,
I wonder in what key the world came to be?

Kathy Culmer

What about for you and me?
Maybe the key of E, for eternity.

(What part of you,
Right now,
By chance,
Does the rhythm of this rhyme
Make your mind, heart,
or spirit dance?)

60

We are being and becoming
Though we ourselves cannot yet see
With eyes
What was beforehand, appointed from eternity,
Envisioned by God, our Maker, before one speck came to be,
Though to us and our imaginings, for now a mystery,
the fabric of our being, being woven skillfully,
willfully and wonderfully,
Painstakingly.

We are being,
and becoming,
Moment
By moment,
Daily,
More and more to see.

Though it does not yet appear what we shall be,
we know with certainty,
with the whole of our being,
we shall be. Eternally.

And when we do see fully and completely,
we shall then see the One in whose image we were made to be.

Amen.

61

What doesn't break us, gives us legs to stand on, knees to bow, and wings to fly.

Sometimes
God is working our legs.

God allows us or assigns us a thing to walk through to help us find or feel or shape our legs.

Sometimes by allowing us to go through what we go through, God is giving us legs to stand on.

Sometimes God is steadying the legs we've been given.

Sometimes God is strengthening our legs so they can hold up and hold us up.

And sometimes God is allowing us to discover the legs we've been given.

Help us to remain steady, O God, even when our legs wobble, or when we can't feel them beneath us, or when we feel them too much.

So they can hold us up, walk us through, and bring us closer to You.

Amen.

62

Sing Anyway

Sometimes in the morning if you're not moving too fast,
You can hear the bird's song loud and clear.

(Note, the birds may be singing whether or not you hear)

This morning amidst the dreariness all around
Neither sunshine nor blue sky anywhere to be found
I heard its sound.

You know, the birds sing any way
They don't get up and say,
"It's cloudy out, so I'm not gonna sing today."

They tweet or chirp or trill their little happy song
And keep right on going along.

We might take a lesson from the carefree bird,
Where no matter the appearance of the day,
Our sweet song could still be heard,
Sunshiny or not, and in spite of the gray,

We would just sing our song anyway.
Which just might chase the gray away.

So go ahead. Sing your song. Sing it anyway.

Whether it's loud and out of tune or can barely be heard.

You never know, if just might lift you up a little higher,
Like it does the bird.

Kathy Culmer

63

Let the words of my mouth
heal and not hurt
help and not hinder
build up and not tear down
be life-giving and not taking
be the truth necessarily spoken and with love
be pleasing and acceptable to You, O Lord!

Our WORDS matter. They have POWER far greater than we can imagine or of which we're aware.

Life and death POWER, to create or destroy, hurt or heal, smooth over or lay bare.

Our WORDS are irretrievable, once released into the air. With such high stakes, it behooves us to take care, with heart and mind to prepare, even cover with prayer.

Our WORDS, before we put them out in the atmosphere.

Amen.

64

Whether on the mountaintop
Or somewhere down below

Whether traveling along the pathway
Where daily I must go

Whether walking beside a stream where quiet waters flow
And soothing winds blow

Or amidst the sea where storm clouds grow
And angry waves roar and billow

Whether resting beneath your shadow
Or wandering from the way you would have me to follow

No matter,
This for sure I know.
You are with me,
Wherever I am,
Wherever I go.

Amen.

65

How did we know we could walk until we took the first step
Or know we could run before it was done?

To fall is for sure
To get up and keep going,
A choice.

But, we must, to endure.
A battle not fought can never be won!

When we dare not and do not,
Fear claims itself victor, before we've begun.

Let no good gift go unclaimed,
No good deed go undone.

Let Faith order our steps so we'll not miss a one
Nor stop short of the finish
Until our race is all run.

Help us keep our gaze fixed on You, Lord,
Our eyes on the prize.

The One
Who before us has gone
Prepared the way

Run the race
And already won!

Thank You and Amen!

Kathy Culmer

66

Faith is the hand that takes hold of me when I am groping in the dark and cannot see.

It is the hand that refuses to let go of me, even when I stall or go along reluctantly.

Faith is the hand that instructs my feet and steadies me.

It is the hand that helps me stand up or stand boldly or stand again after I fall, or to even stand at all.

Faith is a more trustworthy guide than sight could ever be.

For even seeing, we cannot fully see.

Faith will not, nor can it fail to deliver me, leading me/guiding me/or if need be, carrying me, safely to my destiny.

Faith not only shows us what happens when we hold on, but faith lets us know what can happen when we let go. It is the power that helps us to do so.

Amen.

67

You can. Yes, you can. You can start now
And let now be your "from now on"

Let whatever has been holding you down
Or keeping you bound

Become new standing ground
The ground on which you pivot and turnaround

Become upward bound
And find yourself on higher ground.

Yes, you can. You really can.

68

Focus as well as vision will impact what and how well and how far you can see. They can determine where and how you go, how far and how you look at/see right where you are, whether your spirits are high or your feelings low.

Focus decides what you will or won't do. It even decides your will for you. For sure, it will get in your thoughts and affect them too. Focus is the thing that directs your thoughts and thus directs you. It's the thing, above all else, that you're paying attention to. It holds your attention and can also hold you. It can make the little seem too big or the big look small or like nothing at all. Focus is what we center on, and what centers us.

When our focus is off-centered, Lord, it's because it's not on You. But with the right placement (sometimes it might even require a shift or two), it brings everything clearly into view. Sometimes (okay maybe all the time and every time) when my focus is just on me, it limits my vision and won't let me fully see.

So, help me remember, Lord, that I can't see big enough until I focus on You. That's what I need You to help me do. As I go through this day, and all others my whole life through, come what may, don't let my focus get away, not too far any way.

Let it rest upon You in every situation and there let it stay, so I can keep on seeing You, and seeing my way, the best way, Your way.

Thank You and Amen.

69

Why is it that the way is not always given to us or known to us or clear to us or made easy for us? Could it be that it is in our wrangling and our wrestling, in our body and soul searching, that deep truths are revealed, that the greatest mysteries become demystified, and that our deepest desires are brought out of the deep?

Oftentimes, we dismiss that which is too easily found or think that because we came upon it with so little effort, it is of little value. Buried treasure cannot be found unless one first digs. Yet, there is a certain hunger or desire that we must first have, realized or not, rooted in destiny, perhaps, to cause us to dig, to send us seeking, with our whole hearts, so that we may find the once-hidden way, and discover unknown treasure.

70

I am not alone.
You are with me, O God, through my breaking heart,
and breaking points,
Which You will mend.
So they don't fully break, but merely bend
Me into the shape of your making.

I am not alone.
You are with me, O God, through my breathlessness, to lift and revive
me and give me fresh wind.
When fear or sorrow enter in or before burdens can become too
burdensome,
Your comfort to keep You will send.

I am not alone.
You are with me, O God, through friendlessness, or the feel of it, and
despair
You are right there,
As God and guardian and a much-needed friend.

When and wherever need makes itself known,
You send your angels to protect and defend.
On You, for all my needs, I can always depend.
If I would but trust You, my provision You'll send.

I am not alone.
You are with me, O God, through my wandering and wondering,
When I lose my way, or in my lostness go astray
Even then with your love you will attend
And bring me back into the fold again.

I am not alone.
You are with me, O God, through my all and everything
My all in all, from beginning to end

Thank You and Amen!

Kathy Culmer

71

"Stop doubting and believe, "

Doubt sees the mountain as an obstacle it can't get around.
Faith sees the mountain as a way to higher ground.

Doubt sees the valley as a fall from grace.
Faith sees the valley as a resting place —
A necessary stop on the way to the next mountain top.

Doubt sees the difficulty and says, "There is no way out."
Faith says, "God's got this. I don't know what you're talking about."

Doubt sees death as the place where life ends.
Faith sees death as the place where life begins.

Faith sees the circumstance, no matter what, bearing fruit that is good.
Faith knows with certainty what doubt never could imagine or ever would.

Doubt will hold you in captivity.
Faith holds the power to set you free!

Kathy Culmer

72

The sun arose

But the darkness did not go away

Some days it's that way

The clouds linger and won't go away

The rain falls but not from the sky

Drops of sorrow from your own weeping eye

Though you feel you grieve alone

Not so

Heaven's heart does also groan

It too can feel your hurt, your pain,
Bearing it alongside you 'til your strength you do regain
And on your own can carry on.

Then comes dawn,
The sun-Son breaking through,
Showing forth anew,
To swallow up the darkness,
That has kept Love's ever-presence hidden from view.

Blessed be the God who comforts us in our mourning,
and when night has run its course, gifts us with the morning!

Kathy Culmer

73

When I am afraid, I will trust in You.
And when I am not,
I will trust in you too.
When I don't know what to or how to or have the strength to do,
Even then, I will trust in You.

When I can't see my way, Your way, Any way at all, O God,
my Way-maker, I will trust in You.

When my soul is cast down and no peace, no joy can be found,
Even then, I will trust in You.

Not only then,
But even when
I'm feeling my best,
Without worry or stress,
Or being hard-pressed,
And am able to rest and rest-assured.
To see and to say and to know that I am blessed.

When I'm able to rest and rest-assured,
No matter the circumstance, no matter the test
Knowing I'm blessed,
Truly blessed,
Even then, In those times,
I will trust in You too.

Whether feeling despair
Or that I don't have a care,
I will trust in You.
Whatever, O Lord, I am going through,
With Your help, I will ever trust in You!

Kathy Culmer

74

A Little Sunshine for a Cloudy Day
(Cause out of sight doesn't mean it's gone away)

Regardless of how gloomy things may appear
No matter how gray
Hold on!

It's just a matter of time before it's no longer that way.

Not only will the sun come out tomorrow
(maybe even later today)
But it never went away.

People come and go, move in and out of orbit,
Dreariness too that can cloud our view.
But the sun,
Whether or not we see it, is in its place to stay.

And you can count on this truth to be true,
That as surely as night follows day

It's just a matter of time before we once more
see its light shining on a new day.

Kathy Culmer

75

Like air, You are, O God
Though we cannot see You
You are all around and everywhere.

Let us breathe You in deeply, O Lord
Then give release into the atmosphere

Breath into the air
Holy breath
That the breathless too may be aware
Of Your presence
All around and everywhere.

Like water, You are, O God
You quench our thirst
Of body,
And Soul
But partake, we must do first
Let us drink deeply, O Lord
Of your life-giving
Soul-quenching water
Drench us with Your spirit,
In You, let us be immersed.

Like sound, You are, O God
All around
Sometimes imperceptible and sometimes clear.
Whether from the lips of men/women/children,
Or riding whispers of the wind,
Or even from the depths within,
You utter both the simple and profound.

Kathy Culmer

Because we do not hear You, Lord
It does not mean You do not speak,
Or that You do not answer prayer,
When Your answer isn't what we seek.

Help us to listen deeply, O Lord.
To hear
Discern
Whether in the silence or the sound
Your voice, Your will, Your presence
To be found.

Like air, O God, You are always and everywhere
The heavens and the earth declare!

Thank You and Amen!

Kathy Culmer

76

"Blessed are those who hunger...for they shall be filled."
Mt. 5:6

Hunger is a funny thing. God could have made us to never hunger—to want nothing more or nothing different or nothing at all, to be resigned to and satisfied with sameness. But instead, God gave us recurring desire and the need to be filled and filled again. And again.

Had we not been created thus, we would, perhaps, never know the taste of something new or know the kind of desire that rouses us to go in search of, before we settle into what satisfies our palates, so that we may clarify our taste. Or we might not know the sweetness of getting full of one's desire. Without the pangs of hunger, we might never be moved to move beyond our complacency or be stirred to go in search of greater satisfaction. Or we might never partake of the Living Bread that can fill our hunger and save our souls.

What is perhaps most remarkable about hunger, whether for food or fulfillment, or for the ultimate: God, is that it will make us get up and go in search of, with a willingness to pay the required price, until our bellies are full or our souls satisfied.

Breath of God, fill me up anew.
Holy Breath, fill me through and through.
Let me Your presence feel
In the quiet and the still
Let deep speak to deep
As You will
My soul to keep
And longing to fulfill.

Breath of God
Holy Breath
Fill me up anew
Refresh
Revive
Renew
Stir me up
As only You
Can do.

Breath of God
Life-giving breath
Holy breath
Fill your servant
'Til there's no room for more
Except I pour.
Amen.

Kathy Culmer

78

Drinking Life (or Drinking It In),
Some guzzle it so quickly,
They can scarcely swallow or taste it.
When guzzling, you can easily spill or waste it.
(If you don't take it easy, guzzling can leave you unsatisfied and make
you queasy.)

Some sip and savor,
To longer enjoy the taste and flavor,
Not wanting it to be gone too fast.
Wanna get every drop of goodness they can
and make it last.

Some take it in,
In a slow and steady stream,
To quench and satisfy
Deep longings and places that are dry,
Careful not to miss a drop,
Until filled,
And satisfied
Before they stop.

At whatever pace you decide. Drink. Deeply. The waters. Of life.
That your thirst will be quench and your soul satisfied.

79

Help us to remember, O Lord, that though the chaos swirls about us and political storms rage, there is an eye within the center that has power to assuage.

Help us to keep our hearts and eyes focused upon the center.

Help us to hold on to hope and not doubt, then we will not be overwhelmed by unsavory winds that whirl about.

Let us keep our eyes on the Center that can center us and steady us and save us from the storm—the Eye that will help us to see for true.

Help us, O God, to never take our eyes, affections, or hope off of You. See us and be with us all, through it all.

Thank You and Amen.

80

Lord have mercy
Christ have mercy
On the sick
the suffering
the crying
the trying
and those they try
the dying
the sighing
Nobody knows the trouble I see
(Sighing is just singing without the notes)
the cried out
the dried out and tried out
the lied out
and those they've lied to and about.

Lord have mercy
Christ have mercy
On the grieving
those who grieve and will be comforted
and on those who cannot or will not
on the burdened
the weary and dreary
and those full of fear
that cripples and stymies and won't let the fearful see or move beyond.

On the worn and the torn
the lonely and forlorn
the troubled
those who despair
and can't find hope anywhere
Nobody knows like Jesus!

Kathy Culmer

Lord have mercy
Christ have mercy
on those pleading
and interceding
and standing in need
and tending to the needs of the needy
in love and deed
on those for whom life has become too much
and those for whom it is not enough.

Lord have mercy
Lord have mercy
Christ have mercy
On me.
On us.
Mercy to
Stop our trouble from troubling
Or from troubling us.
Amen.

Kathy Culmer

81

Faith confidently says:
"I know that I can touch the sky.
I can't imagine why
I cannot soar that high.
But even if I don't reach that far,
I'm sure that if I keep holding on,
I will land upon a star.
And if I cannot on my own
Climb high enough up on the air,
I know the hands of God will surely lift me there."

Kathy Culmer

82

I used to fall apart
And Love put me back together again and again and again
But then,
Something in my heart and in my head said,
Time has come for this to end
Your doubt grieves me and does offend.
When will you begin
to really trust and not just pretend?
I didn't have to condescend
and die for you to spend
Your life in doubt and fear,
But rather that you know with certainty,

I am
the One
On whom you can depend
My boundless love to comprehend
Its power to transcend!
In the face of every foe
I will defend you
Whatever circumstance in life
May attend you
However great or small
Will never fully apprehend you
Because I am within you
Always!
Child of mine,
Let my Word do its work and amend you,
your thoughts and ways
So I can send you!

Amen.

83

When you plant a seed, you let go of it, and other than water it, there's little else you can do to it to make it grow.

You can't even watch it grow.

You trust that it will.

The next time you see it, it is no longer the seed you put in the ground, but what the seed has grown into, after it has come through the earth in which it was sown. Not unlike prayer. You pray the prayer, and you water it with trust. In confidence, you wait for fruit. Some of us (myself included), for lack of trust sometimes, nearly dig up the seed that we'd planted with prayer. But what we don't know or often enough remember is that we cannot make the seed grow, neither with worry or woe. We can only let it go.

May the seeds of your longing take root, and may you have the peace of knowing as they are growing and becoming fruit.

Amen.

84

"For the mouth speaks what the heart is full of."
Matthew 12:34

Your words will eventually tell on you.

Our words are like clothing.
Some cover.
Some are see-through.
Some, though they cover, still reveal.
We choose them to fit.
And accentuate.
Or, in some instances,
to cover up.

While clothing can hide our truth, temporarily, our words will expose our truth. They will give us away. When we speak, especially when we misspeak, it is like disrobing or undressing in public—whether all at once, piece by piece, or layer by layer—until the once-covered is left standing naked, exposed, with its true self showing, private parts and all.

Take care with your words.

But, more importantly, with the heart that gives them shape.

85

Some birthing requires long and hard labor, lots of pushing and paining, before life can come forth and show. Some growth is stunted because more time is needed for the growing to grow. Some waiting may seem endless because we already received long ago what we'd been looking and hoping for, but because we couldn't see it, just didn't know. Some living never gets lived or not enough, because when opportunity comes knocking they turn it away with a 'no' or refuse to even get up and go open the door.

86

Some of us are full of faith until we are in most need of faith.

She often said she had faith, and she thought that she did,
But when the time of trial came, her faith went and hid.
When she needed her faith the most, she couldn't find it anywhere.
The faith she said and thought she had, just wasn't there.
So, she went to God in prayer.
Lord, she prayed, let my faith be real and not run out on me
I need a working faith with fruit that I can see.

Faith is not about the words you say.
Or even the words you pray.
It's the confident believing that God can and will make a way.
No matter what the need or circumstance, God will be there for you
and with you, come what may!

Kathy Culmer

87

"Weeping may endure for a night, But joy comes in the morning."
Psalm 30:5

Hold on.
Though appearing overcast
Dark skies will not last
The clouds will soon pass.

Winter comes for a reason
But lasts only a season.
Night falls, not to stay
But, in time, to give rise to a new day.

When the dark seems darkest
And you can't see your way
Hold on
Day is on the way.

As surely as night breaks to day
Weeping turns to joy
And death gives way
to eternal life
Light is coming.

Hold on.
Even if it has not yet come into sight,
Be encouraged.
(Remember, morning begins in the middle of the night)
You are coming to the light.

Kathy Culmer

88

EVERY day is a good day.
It's how we look at it that keeps us from seeing it that way.

When I woke up today
I heard the voice in my head or heart or somewhere say,
"Today's gonna be a great day!"
So, I resolved right away
Not to let any tempters get in my way.
One by one, I called out my usual predators,
Before my good day became their prey.
Pity, I said, "You can't come and play.
Doubt, get out; You can't stay.
Frustration, leave me alone, get out of my way.
Procrastination, you won't cause me delay.
Not today, anyway.
Gossip, I'm not gonna let you in, 'cause you'll just betray,
Distort what I hear and misrepresent what I say.
Bitterness, resentment, jealousy and pride,
Y'all need to step aside.
You try to run me like a relay,
But you won't be chasing me or my joy away this day."

Lord, help me to keep any peace-stealers and joy-killers at bay
And other thieves lurking about trying to snatch the good out of my day,
Or trying to get in my head and my space to try and keep me from
seeing it that way.

89

Who else but God?
Who else but God!

Who can make a mountain
Who can fill the sea
Who can grow a seed into a tree
Or whatever it will be?

Who can make all of humanity
making each one of us individually
uniquely
with never another to ever be
exactly the same as you or me?

At best, what human hands can make,
But not create,
is mere facsimile
imitating what God envisioned in eternity
and crafted originally
when all that is,
was coming to be..

Who else but God?
Who else?
But God!
Amen.

Kathy Culmer

90

When young children get a present, they are often as delighted with the wrapping or the container as they are with what's inside. They giggle and coo and play—sometimes it seems all day—with the stuff we throw away. They taste and touch and beat on the stuff that the gift came wrapped in. They show their gratitude that way.

When parents get those little gifts from their children that were hand-made, they mean as much, if not more to us, as anything for which they could have paid. As misshapen or imperfect as they may be, it's the love and pride in it that we see—a gift made by its maker just for me.

When did we get to the point that the gift of the day by itself was not enough? At what age did we start to say that it had to come a certain way to be okay?

What if the gift of each day were received in that way, with delight like the child who finds as much reason to smile or something worthwhile from the gift that's inside as what gets tossed on the pile, and still finds a way to giggle and coo and play any way.

Or, no matter what the day looks like going in it, still finding pleasure and treasure within it, not because of its appearance but the love that went in it and that we got to be in it.

What if every day, just because we were given the gift, we would rejoice and be glad anyhow, anyway?

91

It is easy to get stuck. It is a whole lot easier to get stuck than to get unstuck. I backed my car in some mud and almost instantly I was stuck. It took me one gentle press on the gas pedal to get stuck in the mud, but a whole lot of wheel spinning and mud-splattering to get out.

Sometimes you get stuck because of a choice you've made. Sometimes because you do nothing to keep from getting stuck. Sometimes because you weren't paying attention or didn't look where you stepped. Sometimes because you get too comfortable. There are lots of reasons we get stuck in the mud, in a job, in unhealthy relationships, in our thinking, our ways, our work, our lives, in the past.

You can get stuck by simply doing nothing or doing nothing different, or by staying in the same place and doing the same thing for too long. You can even be stuck and not know you are stuck until you try to move or move on. One thing for sure, you will have to work a whole lot harder to get yourself free from the thing that's holding you than you did to fall into its grips.

When you realize you are stuck or that you are on the way to being stuck, whatever you do, don't keep doing what you've been doing all along. Try something new. Don't look back. Focus on what's in front of and not behind you, wherever it is you want to go.

If you have to, get help to pull or push or guide you through, or to give you a hand in getting the gum off your shoe.

92

Color Blinds

What if God had said, "Let us make humans in our own image and likeness, and let us make them all the same, just package them differently (packaging them in different shapes and sizes and colors and gifts and languages), and then not tell them?"

What if God left the unwrapping for us to do? Left it to us to get inside and make the discovery of our sameness ourselves?

Then, as the packages are opened and the wrappings and trappings are removed, as barriers of separation are shattered or defied or discounted, we would come to know each other more and more, and even know God more and more, and we would come to recognize more of our sameness? Could God have been thinking this all along when God made us in the beginning? Could this be what some humans have feared all along?

Beauty—it comes in a myriad of colors, through which God sends his grace.

When we look deep enough within (beyond the covering of skin, the sweetness of the fruit is found therein)

We can see (Help us, O God, to look long enough and deeply enough to see) God's face.

Amen.

93

We were not random acts, you see,
Though we may act randomly.

None of us!

That is not how we came to be.

Planned, purposed and love-crafted, were we
Every one of us, intentional.

Equipped to fulfill a destiny
Conceived before time began in eternity
With potential and power to fulfill

And be fully filled
And we will

When this truth
This reality
We can see —
A truth that
Indisputably
Undeniably
Irrevocably
sets us free —
When we believe it,
Accept it,
And live our lives accordingly.

Amen.

94

Bend But Don't Break

A prayer so that we won't so easily get bent out of shape, to help us avoid crippling rigidity and fraying edges, and to keep us from reaching our breaking points:

Blessed are the flexible for they shall bend and not break or get bent out of shape.

While being firm can be an asset, a mattress sleeps a whole lot better if it's got a little give in it. The tree that breaks is the one that does not bend in the face of a mighty wind. Lord, in your mercy,
help us to be flexible enough to bend, where needed, but not break; to stretch beyond injury where peace and pardon are at stake; to reshape old visions so of greater ones we can partake; and, where reasonable, to be willing to relinquish good for better's sake.

Thank You and Amen.

95

I did not ask for the sunrise
But You gave it anyway
It came with Your gift of a new day.

I did not ask for air
Sleeping or waking
It was already there
All around and everywhere.

I did not ask for what my heart desired most
You gave that too.
You knew.
You always do!

God's grace and goodness give us not only what we ask for
But knowing,
Every day, provides so much more.

Thank You, Lord, for all that You've given
That I asked for
And thank You, too, for the so much more!

Thank You and Amen.

Kathy Culmer

96

O what a relief it is when you become aware
That you do not have to force your circle into a square.
After all the time and energy you've spent!
That you don't have to become misshapen and bent
trying to fit into a shape for which you were never meant.

What freedom when you can just be content knowing that your circle,
or whatever shape you find best suited to be, suits you perfectly.
That it was with intent and loving care
That you were shaped into a circle and not a square.
That you color just fine
Even when it is outside the line.
That your shape and what you instinctively do
Are no aberration but are by Divine design
A part of your Creator's master plan for you.
Oh what a joy when you can finally see
And celebrate
(It's never too late)
Your beautiful self
As you were created to be!

97

Made in God's image, yet being and becoming, shaped, formed, fashioned into God's likeness, more and more of God in me. It does not yet appear what I/we shall be—fearfully, wonderfully made perfectly, yet being and becoming perfected, as more and more God shapes and takes shape in me. Making us to be what we cannot yet comprehend or fully see. Envisioned by God long before we ever came to be, more and more, and more of God in me, 'til God in me should be and see, and be seen. Planned and purposed so to be since before time and time again and throughout all eternity. Amen.

Kathy Culmer

98

Favor opens doors. Grace carries us through.

Mercy shows us the door once more in case we missed it before.

For the time and time again, when,

Thank You and Amen.

99

Transformation is not an easy thing, nor is it done hurriedly. It is what you have to go through to get from where you were and are to what you were always intended to be. Time is required to reshape a thing ne-ces-sar-i-ly. Fruit must grow and ripen before you can taste and see. The caterpillar must press through before it can fly into its destiny. Likewise, the Potter must keep on forming and transforming 'til the image He can see, in His hands, in His time, is the you., is the me. We were meant to be. Help us, O God, even while we are becoming, to bear witness to You, then, to keep on bearing witness while we're living into.

Thank You and Amen!

100

When I was growing up my mother would often send me to the corner store, just two doors from our house. Many times after she'd told me what to get she would say, "Bring me back my change." But some days when I returned from the store, she'd say, "You can keep the change." I loved those days. Sometimes I'd spend it right away; sometimes save it for another day.

Ever feel like sometimes God blesses you and says, "And you can keep the change?" Like God says, "I know you asked for one thing, but I'm gonna throw in some extra and let you have the change." And when you do, what do you do with the change?

Now unto God who is able to, and who does, pay for our cart full of good things, some that we didn't even have on the list when we went shopping, with change left over, and Who tells us to keep the change (Ephesians 3:20).

And while I don't always see it that way or know how I'm gonna pay, my cart is full, and my pocket is heavy with change.

101

Growing and Becoming
Isn't a mountain just a rock that grew and grew and grew
Until it grew into
Something bigger
Something more
than it ever imagined
or could on its own do?
The same is true for you.
You could do that too,
Become a mountain if you want or will allow yourself to.
That possibility lies within you
Not to become something so big that you obstruct the view
Or stand in the way of others becoming
Or doing what they seek/strive/desire to do
But so you can lift them up
elevate their aspirations and broaden their view
Perhaps even showing them the way
They can reach new heights too.
If you just believe and allow yourself to
You too could be like the rock that grew and grew
Until you grow into
Something bigger
Something more
than you ever imagined,
Something far beyond the limitations life tried to impose on you.

102

Curb our appetites, O God, for ungodly things—ViolenceGreedSelf-CenterednessSelf-RighteousnessOverindulgenceComplacency—Make them so undesirable to us that they become stench in our nostrils, so distasteful to us that they become bitterness in our mouths. Let sin and evil and acts of violence be so indigestible to us that we choke on the mere thought of them and vomit out their possibilities. Deliver us from evil, O Lord, and from making excuses for the evil we cause, and the evil we allow. Your Word tells us that You are faithful and just to forgive us and cleanse us of unrighteousness when we ask and confess it to You. But You can't do anything with the unrighteousness that we hold on to.

Curb our appetites, O God, for ungodly things. Give us new cravings instead. Let them and the filling of these desires become our daily bread. JusticeMercyLovePeaceForgivenessGenerosityGoodwill. Let these be the fruit that we crave, our souls to save, fruit that will fill us and grow us and bear seed in us—a planting of the Lord to display God's splendor through us.

Comfort those, this day O Lord, who have suffered grief and loss and hurt because of our unbridled passions and unwholesome desires and our actions or inactions because of them. Heal them and us, O Lord! Amen!

Kathy Culmer

103

A Reflection on Psalm 19

The heavens declare the glory of God,
The skies, the work of His hands, proclaim.
Earth's beauty with all its varied terrain,
Communicates joyously and without words
A message much the same!
There is no place above the earth
Where there is no sky
It is all the time and everywhere.
No matter where we stand in open air
The sky is there.
There is no place under the sky
Where earth is not there.
It is all the time and everywhere.
Whether or not we can see
Above or buried beneath the sea
Whether ocean floor or dry land
It is the ground upon which we stand.
There is no place
Outside or inside time and space
Where God is not
No matter how big or small the spot.
Though we cannot see all of God
Or God all at once
Like earth and sky and even air
God is all the time and everywhere.
In the sky, on the earth, God's handiwork is seen
Above, below and in between.
The heavens declare
The earth proclaims
All living things the same
God is.
All the time and everywhere!
Amen.

Kathy Culmer

104

Even though we walk through the valley—Yes, sometimes we must, even though we don't want to, go there—Help us, O God, to see You in our valley-places the in-between spaces as we did on the mountain top, to realize that though the valley is a necessary drop, it is a temporary stop on the way to the next mountain top. Let us from our valley-view come to really see and to know more of You, for true. Help us to know for ourselves that just as You are with us on the mountain top, You will be with us in the valley, too. Our feet, You have made to be like that of the deer. Give us the sure-footedness to climb, dear Lord, to scale the heights and the steadfastness to stand, that we may dwell on our high places with You. With thanksgiving we pray, O God. Amen.

105

God Will Bring You Through

I have learned and know for true
That there is not one day, one season, one circumstance that God has
brought me to
That God has not brought me through.
Yesterday cannot keep hold of you
Unless that's what you let it do.
Every time our tomorrow becomes our today, once more we have made
it through.
And what appears to us that we have not yet made it through,
We're one day closer to.

Kathy Culmer

106

Things to leave behind (In order to move forward):

Things that weigh me down and keep me in the blind.
Things that keep me from getting, keeping and enjoying all the good
that could be mine.

Procrastination, it's such a waste of time.
Clutter gets in my way and makes me hard to find.
Anger steals my joy and robs me blind.
Jealousy won't let me appreciate what is already mine.
Unforgiveness tempts me to malign, keeps me always in a bind
In time, my own soul to undermine.
Doubt and worry (=stress) cloud my view
keep the light from getting through
Can even cause a health decline.
Fear does nothing but confine.
Negativity won't let me see the good right in front of me causes me to
whine and pine
Drives me out of my own mind.
Guilt has got to flee. It keeps a hold on me, holds me captive by the
past, no matter what won't let me pass, Presses my hold button and
keeps me stuck on rewind.
Indecision is where I need to draw the line.
Leaving any one or more of these behind
Without a doubt will help me find
More joy and more peace of mind.

107

A butterfly isn't born in such a beautiful state
But must wait
It must go through the things that caterpillars do and grow into
Before what it will be comes fully into view.
For us the same is true
We must go through
Some necessary journey ourselves to grow into
To become
Until the fullness of our beauty and being comes into view.
All the while in the hands of the One who is lovingly molding and
shaping us into.

108

"The heavens declare the glory of God,
the skies proclaim the work of the Divine Designer's hands."
Psalm 19:1

Some days it appears that God rolls back the clouds and lets us watch Him work on the canvas of the skies, whether with sweeping stroke or one blotch at a time, or with some other design, the Artist rendering an artful display of a glorious new day. Then there are those times when it looks like God opens our eyes and lets us watch Him work on the canvas of our lives, seeing them take shape, in a new light or a new way. Sometimes in the morning, we see it best, or in the evening as we are preparing for the night's rest. Time of day may have no say, at all. Perhaps, it is simply the Spirit's call, our state of heart and mind, our openness to see and not the time.

Amen.

109

Those People

About those people who you just can't stand or are sick and tired of, who you don't want to be bothered with or bothered with anymore (even when they are your kin or your friends, especially when they are your kin or your friends or who might otherwise be).

What if it is your assignment from God to learn how to love imperfect people? What if that's the reason God keeps putting them in your pathway and bringing them to you? And if you don't know how already —if it's not a natural thing for you to do—then to learn how to. Not to fix them, but to love them. People who just can't seem to get it right, whether because they can't or won't. People who have to be told or shown the same thing over again and again and again. You know, people like you. People who make it hard for you to love them. People who feel they don't deserve to be loved. People who don't know how to love you back. And some who never will. What if God intentionally gave this assignment to you, in addition to all the other wonderful and life-changing things you will do. To make and shape you so that others could see Him in you and you could be an example of that kind of loving for them too. What if God put you in close proximity to those imperfect, hard-to-love people to grow you and challenge you to do, what you would not otherwise do, to teach you how to love others as He loves you. To stir up the best in and bring the best out of you. What if the what-if's were true? What difference would it make to you?

110

Note to self:

Love your enemies. Pray for those who despitefully use you, done wronged you or pissed you off or whom you just generally can't stand or stand the thought of praying for, And if you cannot yet bring yourself to pray or pray and mean it, then pray for your own soul until you can. Amen.

111

If God has forgiven and delivered you,
And especially if you know that to be true,
Maybe it's time for you
To let go of the anger, bitterness, and resentment
That you've been holding onto
Or that's been holding onto you.
Maybe God made the ultimate sacrifice for you
Because God knew
That holding onto stuff like that
Would be the death of you.

112

Wondering Eyes

No matter where I am in the world, it is the same sky that covers me. Yet, I cannot see it in its entirety. With eyes alone I can only see partially, and imperfectly, that which is in front of me or near in proximity. Where I am and where I stand determines what in the world I see, and how, and with what clarity. Same as with eternity. Only in part can we see 'til through God's eyes, we see more perfectly.

113

Friendship

This about friendship I've found to be true
The true ones are the ones who will stick with, stand beside, and stand
up for you.
And no matter what it is you are going through
They're not there just watching but going through with you.
They will see you at your worst
Hope for you the best
And no matter what the circumstance
Love you none the less.

114

You are blessed and beautiful, and oh, so loved! You are a jewel in the King's crown, the sparkle in His eye, the high note in His song (though you have not yet reached it, He is holding it there for you), and you are the rhythm of His heartbeat. You are your Creator's beloved and best! May you experience God's love in a special way today, feel the comfort of His warm embrace, see His face in all you meet today, and may others see His face in you. May you hold others with the same regard as your Beloved holds you. Amen.

115

Keep Your Eyes Open

We carefully guard our possessions, that is, our stuff. We put locks on, install security systems and keep watch so thieves can't get in and take our stuff–the material things we have accumulated or assigned value to–away. But there are other thieves we just open ourselves up to–thieves like anger, bitterness, resentment, unforgiveness, pride, jealousy, and the like–and let them walk right in the door and do what they do.

If thieves attempt to rob our property, we take swift action to get them out and chase them away. But, if it's a thief that seeks to rob us of our peace, too often we let them stay and give them the chance they're looking for to rob us blind, take away our joy, laughter, relationships, and our peace of mind.

Let us be careful and prayerful, then, knowing that these things are out there always lurking about, and make sure we do everything we can to keep them out.

116

The mountain that looms before me, O God, is SO BIG
I don't know what to do
Its other side seems an impossible place to get to.
Its height is so great, I can't see its peak
In the face of this mountain, I feel helpless and weak.
Its expanse is so wide, I can't see my way round
With no strength, no courage, and no vision of my own, to be found
I don't know how I will ever get off the ground.

The climb is too steep;
Should I fall, it's too deep.
Its rock is too hard,
Its edges too sharp,
Its slopes have no guard, no grip
I might fall; I might slip.
Its roads are narrow and winding, I could easily lose my way
Maybe I should go ahead and try any way.

I don't know. I am tempted. Fear tells me to stay.
Where it's safe or at least it appears that way.
This mountain's too big; there's no way I can climb!
While its height is most daunting,
Its reach is sublime.

Although it looks immovable, impenetrable, and impassable from where
I now stand
From Your vantage, Lord, it's just a pebble You could hold or toss, I know,
with Your hand.
So, in the face of this or any other mountain where by chance or
circumstance I find myself thrust,
Give me all that is needed to do what I must, and help me, O God, to
climb and to trust!

Kathy Culmer

117

Why do we fear the giant when we know the Giant Slayer? God knew we would go there; that's why God gave us prayer.

> *"We should go up and take possession of the land,*
> *for we can certainly do it"*
> Num. 13:30

Fear and doubt see the giant as a thing that can't be beat, and so they seek retreat. The giant is too big, they say and run away. But Faith sees God when some giant we meet. It knows that with God's help, the giant will suffer defeat. The eyes of faith will see and show that the giant is a conquerable foe.

Giants may look daunting but are rarely as unconquerable as they appear to be. They just seem that way when we only trust in what we can see. In the face of Faith the giant must flee or risk destruction or captivity. Faith trusts the unseen and is confident that the Trusted One will give us victory.

When the giant stands in our way, O God, help us to see and put our trust in You, our giants to slay. Strengthen us to take a stand, go in and take possession of our promised land, anyway. Thank You and Amen.

118

Pride is like looking face forward in a mirror and not seeing all of you. Then, looking in a rear view mirror and all you see is you. No matter what, pride will always give you a distorted view of you and of others too. If you want to see yourself for true and pride gets in the way when you're looking at you, you may just have to make an adjustment or two, not to the mirror, but to you.

119

Bitter Fruit

She used to be beautiful and bright
'Til bitterness came and took her light
Convinced her that life wasn't treating her right
She bought into the lie, and now this is her plight.

Bitterness can make you look like someone unrecognizable to others
and even to you
Make you look like and act like someone you never knew,
Or wanted to.
Bitterness itself used to be something else
(Anger, disappointment, failure, unforgiveness, love without requite or
not quite)
Then left alone, it grew and before anyone could tell or knew,
Whatever it once was had turned to spite.
When left alone to grow, that is what these things will do,
Change themselves into something else and change you, too.

It can hamper your vision and cripple your sight
Rob you of your will and take your might
With its bitter lies, told subtly, at first, then outright,
Distorting the truth so you no longer have strength or the desire to fight,
Or take flight.

Bitterness will try and hold you captive from within and without
Won't let anybody else get in and won't let you get out
While on your own, you cannot this battle win
There is a power you hold within
And it alone can break the bond of bitterness' captivity.
Bitterness, you see, has an enemy
From which it cannot flee.

Love, and love alone can defeat bitterness and set you free
Love can once more make things right
Return you from darkness and the night
Give you back your beauty and your light.

(But beware: Bitterness will try and hold on tight; it will not let go of you
without a fight. But try with all your might to let love come to light.)

120

What if?

This is the day that the Lord has made all fresh and new. What if today we did something fresh and new, too? What if we try something new, think about or do something in a way we aren't used to? It just might be what we need to do to get out of the habit/routine/rut of doing and thinking that because we've always done it one way, there's no other way for us to do?

What if we try a new route? Go another way, or out of our way? And, although we've always done it that way, what if we tried it this way—a new way? What if we looked at some folks again and in a new way, real hard, perhaps someone we had written off before to see if we could see something more, maybe even the God in them and see what a difference it might make in them and us?

What if? What if all that really matters is that we love God with all our heart and mind and soul and strength and not how we do it or what we look like doing it, but as the Spirit leads us to, even when that Spirit leading doesn't look like what we expect it to?

What if? We would venture beyond levels of comfort to seek God in ways fresh and new, or look at, see, and treat others in new ways too? Who knows what amazing discoveries and insights that would lead us to, if we would dare to do something new or in a way we're not accustomed to.

121

"Now He who provides seed for the sower
and bread for food will provide and multiply your seed
for sowing and increase the harvest of your righteousness."
2 Cor. 9:10 (AMP)

Grow us, O God, grow in us. Grow us up, grow us into. May our roots grow deeper into the soil of Your desire, our branches wider in their stretch and upward and outward in their reach. Bless our fruit to be filling and satisfying and plentiful—plenty-full of the sweetness and goodness and likeness of its Sower and Source. Amen!

122

Help me to hear you, Lord, in the raindrops, in the tree tops, in the life stops and goes, in the silence, through the noise, when the wind blows, what it knows, whatever your choice, it's your voice, be it black and white or gray, whatever the way, help me to discern what you say.

Amen.

123

My GPS gave me a message once, actually more than once, that said, "entering unverified territory." I shared that once with a group during a talk, and they laughed out loud and said, "You must have been really lost." Nobody I tell that to seems to have ever gotten that message on their GPS before, but it really did say that. Granted, I am directionally challenged, but even I was taken aback by getting such a message from my GPS.

The way I figured, it could have been an indication of a couple of things: how lost I was, or that I was traveling a road that had not been travelled enough for its way to be known.

Sometimes in life, we can find ourselves wandering into unverified territory. Perhaps you have been there once before, maybe even more. Sometimes we may find ourselves there because we have not followed the directions we were given, and sometimes we find ourselves there because that's where the directions led us. My GPS shuts up while I am driving in unverified territory. It does not tell me when and where to turn or even if I should turn around. It is silent. If you have gone there, then you know the silence of which I speak. When you enter unverified territory, you must rely on your internal guide to help you navigate the terrain, to find your way and ultimately to lead you out of unfamiliar places back onto a known way. For some, perhaps, you could say you were called to verify the territory.

124

Help me, O God, to remember,
Even when I can't see You,
You are still there.
When I can't feel You,
You still care.
When I can't hear You,
You haven't gone anywhere.
When Your answer is a long time in coming,
Not to despair.
That You are the God of my every when, my all-the-time and my
everywhere.

Thank You and Amen!

125

"Forgive, and you will be forgiven."
Luke 6:37

Small particles when unattended can accumulate, harden and eventually clog your drain, first slowing the flow then cutting it off completely until nothing can pass through. That's what anger, bitterness and resentment can do to you. They can harden and clog your drain so that love or life cannot freely flow through.

Forgiveness is like doing a detox.
It's what you can do to flush the impurities out of you.
It's an action you take, a decision you make
For your own health's sake.

Although it's not easy and you don't always want to
Sometimes you've just got to do the painful and difficult and painfully difficult to do.
Let go of the thing you've been holding onto
(or that's been holding onto you)
Before it settles into and hardens you.
Periodically, you need to make amends to cleanse.

To forgive is to set free.
Unforgiveness holds the unforgiver in captivity.
Forgiveness is the key that sets the unforgiver free.
Forgive as you have been forgiven
And you will be twice set free.

126

Good seasoning, applied correctly and in the right amount, enhances flavor, brings out the best taste, stimulates appetite to savor not devour in haste, that nothing to be consumed might be lost, or go to waste.

Use me, O God, let me like good seasoning be, poured out from the Master Chef's hand most aptly, my words, my gifts, my actions, all to Your taste, that I might add flavor and that none should go to waste.

Thank You and Amen!

127

A Rainy Day Musing

It has been said and thought and wondered about, if the rain that falls from the sky could possibly be tears falling from God's eye, Science and reason would say it's a lie. No way could raindrops be tears falling from the sky. I just hope that if that's the reason why, the cause was not I, unless, of course, it was because I brought Him so much joy it brought tears to His eye or I made Him laugh so hard, until it made Him cry.

128

This is the day that the Lord has made.
It is a gift and not a given.
Our thank you is in the living.
All are given the same amount of time each day
To spend as we choose and in our own way.
Whether on work, rest, or play
Or whatever the chosen way
It's with our time that we pay.

At the end of the day
Whether or not we paid a fair price,
only we can say.
Precious time!
Be careful how you spend it.
Though it costs us by the minute
The value of each one is determined
By the living we put in it.
Help us, O God, to spend wisely and well, rejoice and be glad in it! Amen.

Kathy Culmer

129

Just for Fun

I think I'll have a yellow day today. I'm feeling kinda sunny, and I want to keep it that way. I'm not feeling blue, and I don't want to. Neither do I wanna wear gray. Even the sky didn't choose that color today. Wouldn't it be something if it were up to us to decide what color we would wear/be each day. What if, just like choosing the clothes we wear, we could pick the color of our day and wear it that way?

130

A prayer for those too weary to weep, too weak to cry, or even try, or keep trying. Let us pray for ourselves and one another, and to be willing where and when we can to offer a lifeline or be one.

Lord, in Your mercy, hear our prayer.

Someone needs a lifeline today, O God
There are voices crying in the wilderness but making no sound
With soul's desperate and agonizing plea to be unbound.
Lord have mercy!

There are too many who have drifted far from the shore
Who are clinging to life in a place where they cannot see land anymore
Treading in waters unnavigable and unknown
Too treacherous and life-threatening to survive on their own
Gasping for air and clinging to life in the dark and murky waters of the deep
They cannot imagine a way back home
Or find rest for their souls to keep.
Lord have mercy on their souls
And send them rescue!
Help them to hold on even when they cannot see a thing to hold on to.

Intervene, O Lord, please don't let the waters overwhelm them and drag them down
Or them become too weary to keep striving and with no strength left go under and drown.
Send them a lifeline, a much-needed hand.
You know, O Lord, the hand they need.
To grip them and hold them and bring them back to the safety of dry land.
Then, help them to go on from there,

Lord, in Your mercy, hear our prayer!
Amen.

Kathy Culmer

131

It is hard to learn anything new, change your perspective or point of view, or to do better the things that you do, when you're the only one talking, or the only one you're listening to.

132

Just because God is silent, or appears to be, doesn't mean that God's not speaking. You know how your mother would give you that "look" and didn't have to open her mouth, but you knew exactly what she was saying, even when you would try and not make eye contact so you wouldn't have to know, so you wouldn't have to face the truth, or face her? Well, sometimes it's in the not-saying that the most can be said.

Could it be that sometimes God speaks that way? That it is in God's apparent silence that God speaks the most profound, without making a sound, 'cause what goes without saying is often best heard without saying a word and to speak it out loud would just be redundant? 'You know it's so, because you've heard it before, and sometimes "the look" says it all.

Kathy Culmer

133

Keeping Pace

There comes a time in life when you have to adjust your pace.
Time and circumstance make that the case.
Doesn't mean you're out of it or no longer a contender in the race…
Just that you've got to run it at a different pace.
Yay!!!
By grace
You're still in the race!
(Rejoice that the race is not done
and you can still run.)
So embrace your pace
Adjust your stride
And enjoy the ride.
Amen.

134

You, O God, are my Source of Plenty. In You, there is no scarcity. What looks like little or nothing to me, You can multiply abundantly. Who can begin to fathom Your capacity, or ability, or generosity? It is endless. You not only can, but desire to provide for me, and through me, far beyond what I can reason or see. It makes no earthly sense to me. How could it be that when I give to others from my own bounty, I don't run out? I still have plenty! Only in God's economy is it so that the more I give away, the more comes back to me. How awesome, O God, that with You as our source and supply, our coffers will never run dry. You keep us full, and we will never be empty!

135

The Lord is my Shepherd,
Though sometimes I forget.
All my needs have been, will be, and are even now, being met.
Even where I have not seen the manifestation yet
I can rest assured knowing before it's even showing
Fulfillment will come
In time
The appointed time
A time already set.

To places of rest the Shepherd will guide me
Through darkness walk beside me
Comfort and peace He'll provide me
In the arms of His shelter, He will hide me
In Him, no matter what, I can confide
His love and faithfulness cannot be denied
I in Him and He in me forever will abide.

Yes, because the Lord is our Shepherd
The Great Shepherd
The Good Shepherd
The Shepherd who never lost a one of His flock
His life laid down in wretched sleep
For the sake of His beloved sheep
Our souls, our lives, our all, to keep,
Yes, because
We need not worry, doubt or fret
For the needs of the Shepherd's beloved sheep
Will always be met.

Kathy Culmer

136

May God speak peace to the storms that rage about us and within us.

Speak peace to the chaos, Lord, Your world where the madness continues to swirl. Speak peace to the chaos, Lord, call back order to Your world. Where reason lies sleeping and weary ones weeping. Mend our brokenness, and broken-heartedness so much in need of repair. Breathe fresh breath upon us, cleanse and clear the air. Help us to b-r-e-a-t-h-e in Your breath so we don't choke on despair.

The world and all that's in it are in your hand. Turn the upside down, right-side up again. Make the staggering and stumbling to once more firmly stand, as You and You alone can!

Speak peace to the chaos, O Lord, within us and round about us, and even in the world beyond us. Let its chastening winds not consume us or entomb us. As in the beginning when You spoke Your "Let-it-be," speak once more and bring back tranquility. Though peace may not mean that all that surrounds us is still, may we, like the eye of the storm, find ourselves and our peace within the center of Your Will. And there, in spite of all that rages about us, to be still and know that You are God!

Thank You and Amen!

137

Some Randomness

Sometimes I feel like a word
Spoken aloud,
But not always heard.

Sometimes a word,
Yet to be spoken
In thought being tossed about,
Awaiting an opportune time to get out
On the breath of a whisper
Or the wings of a shout.

Sometimes,
I feel like a word spoken loud and clear
Heard by all who needed to hear.

Then there are times,
I feel like an unarticulated word
That never shall from lips part
Because it is best kept close to the heart.

Kathy Culmer

138

To See or Not See at All

Sighted means the ability to see
But not with eyes necessarily.
Some seeing with eyes, still cannot fully see.
Blindness does not always mean that with the eyes only you cannot see
or see fully
But sometimes that you cannot fully see.
Short-sighted means to see limited possibility.
Near-sighted sees only what's in front of me.
Far-sighted means the farther away the better I see, but don't get too
close to me.
Half-sighted sees only partially
Keen-sighted the imperceptible with clarity
Fore-sighted, what has yet to come to be.
Hind-sighted, what's already behind me.
Clear-sighted, with or without eyes, sees sharply and accurately

Could it be, then, that one can be sighted and still not see or see only
partially or be blind and fully see?

139

One Under the Sun/Son

Though many, we are one
Under the same sun
Out of earth's dust we came the same
Yet not the same.
Not a one is not covered by the same sky
Or seen by the same loving and watchful eye.
Still, all must someday die
Not all at once, but once for all.
Though many, we are one
Under the same Son
Our oneness in the One
Some may shun
Salvation's gift for everyone.

Kathy Culmer

140

*"Perseverance must finish its work so that you may
be mature and complete, not lacking anything!"*
James 1:4

To see a thing to the finish—to see the thing through—till you've made
the most of the thing or it's made the most of you!

Without perseverance, a cake will not rise;
A seedling will never become a tree unless it tries and tries
Nor the bird leave its nest to reach its destiny in the skies.

What if the earth only rotated half way,
What would happen to the rest of the day?
The day could not move forth from the dawn
It would just have to stay.

If it had not reached its goal,
The frog would have remained forever a tadpole.
The majestic mountain could never hope to be more than a rock or a
hill
Nor the ocean ever more than a stream
If they hadn't kept on growing or flowing and just remained still.

Fruit will not ripen,
And the flower cannot bloom
The butterfly will never take flight unless and until it emerges from its
cocoon.

Beauty, Flight, and all kinds of potential may never be fully realized if we
don't see the thing to the finish and give up too soon.

Without perseverance,
Some things will fall short and others go on way too long,
Seemingly never reaching an end,
So that one might reach its fulfillment and a new thing can begin!

Kathy Culmer

141

All our needs He attends.
Our broken places He mends.
From attack He defends
And our fears apprehends.

For our asking, time and time again
He pardons and cleanses us all from our sins.
Grace upon grace for our sakes He extends.
In time of our troubles, His mercy He lends.

For His will to be done here on earth, He commends us.
With His Word and His Spirit, He equips us and sends us.

Glory to God!
Whose power transcends and Whose love never ends!

Kathy Culmer

142

Worry is the sweaty palm that slaps you senseless, the hand, white-knuckled with fear, that can choke the breath and mobility out of you, the tension-filled arm that distances you with doubt, pushing you farther and farther away from the One—the only One who can snatch you from its grip and get you out. Faith, on the other hand, stretches itself heavenward to make its request, then rests on its back to receive its reward. Worry ties your hands in the battle. Faith gives you the victory.

143

A Closer Look

We are struck first by what we see. We cannot help but be. We rely upon the eye to tell us what we ought to buy. But trusting only the eye can make you buy the lie, and cost you everything. Paradise was lost, and that, at least, in part was why. But even now with fruit, in spite of sight, you squeeze or might, before you take the first bite. The cover on the book does not the whole story tell, but is designed to make it sell. But when it comes to one another, too often we don't want to bother to take a closer look to see beyond the skin, to discover what's within, or dare say, to see them as a friend.

Kathy Culmer

144

"He has tested you to know what was in your heart,
He has caused you to hunger,"
(Deut. 8:3)

Hunger is not a welcome thing, but it is a necessary thing. We need the pangs of hunger to get our attention, to call us back from whatever good or other things with which we are pre-occupied in order to take care of the needs of our bodies and our beings. HUNGER causes us to re-focus. We need the grumblings and rumblings of HUNGER to remind us that we are not totally self-reliant, that we must rely on sustenance from outside ourselves and that we, at certain intervals, must be replenished to stay full or full enough. We need the emptiness of HUNGER to remind us of what we are in need of, of what we are missing. HUNGER helps us to identify our appetites, cultivate our tastes, and clarify our longings. We need HUNGER to move us and motivate us and not leave us alone until we have found food that will not only fill our stomachs but feed our souls.

145

"In whose hand is the life of every living thing,
And the breath of all humankind?"
Job 12:10

For the hands that wake me and rock me and nudge me and stroke me and poke me and hold me and shape me and shield me and wield me and beckon me and embrace me and correct me and lift me and carry me, hands that can catch me and keep me from falling or set me upright on my feet again, hands that have me engraved on their palms, that hold on to me and will never let go of me,

Thank You and Amen.

Kathy Culmer

146

Praise God Anyway

Even when the sky is gray
The sun will shine another day
Praise God any way.

Even when you don't know the words to say
Words are not the only way
Praise God anyway.

Even when you're not feeling it that day
Or feeling some kind of way
Praise God anyway.

Sing or shout or dance or pray
In silence, let your heart have its say
You can praise God your way
Anyway.

For blessings past and those on the way
For grace received we can never repay
And love that never fails no-how, no-way
Praise God anyway.

Because God can and will and Is
Yesterday, today and every day
Praise God anyway!

Kathy Culmer

147

I was busy being anxious and in a hurry for the car sitting in the intersection to get going so I could move into its spot. When the car finally moved out of my way, I was able to see what the driver ahead of me had already seen. There were barriers in the road and a partial lane shutdown which was affecting the traffic flow. Patience is a virtue we can only learn by waiting and is best facilitated by learning to trust the Driver out in front of you Who can see ahead of you, Who, from start to finish, can see your journey through, Who can see the potholes, road blocks, lane closures and other potential barriers and obstructions or entanglements that might trip you up or that might get in your way and cause you delay, or dismay, then can release you for travel when the way has been cleared and it is safe for you to proceed on your way.

How reassuring to know that Someone has already seen the way, made a way, prepared the way, will show you the way, help you find your way, accompany you along the way, and be with you all the way. Yes, it is good to know there is a way, always, and to know the Way-maker who always knows.

148

What do you need to empty out so that you can pour or pour more? What is clogging the pores of your vessel keeping more from getting out or getting in, or getting to you? Whether seen as half empty or half full, the glass has room for more and more to pour. A glass, after all, is for pouring not for storing, into our own thirstiness or some other's. Perhaps the half-glass came to its state because it had been busy being used, being emptied of itself, because being too full of itself would just leave it bloated and feeling full.

Don't get drunk on the things of the world that can clog your pores and cloud your reason, but drink deeply of God's Spirit so that the Spirit's fruit can grow in you and living waters flow out of you.

149

Better get up and get out of bed.
Thoughts won't let me rest;
They just keep rolling around in my head.
Thinking themselves out loud without a word being said.
(Reminding me that I'm still alive and not, well, you know…)
And that's good news!

Getting up and out of bed,
Well, waking up period
Is a thing to celebrate,
Not dread.
Reason enough not to waste a minute of the day ahead
And to live every bit of it that I can instead.

Amen.

Kathy Culmer

150

Snatching Cookies

"For the thief comes to snatch and to take away,"
John 10:10

Back in grade school, sometimes there would be those bully kids who wanted to take your cookies, or your candy bar or your lunch, who just wanted to take your stuff. Sometimes they'd come right up and snatch whatever it was; other times, they'd begin with a little public humiliation, calling you out in front of people, forcing you into surrender. Then other times, they might jump out from a hidden place and take you by surprise. Sometimes you'd give 'em what they wanted just so they'd leave you alone, unaware that what they were really after was not your stuff, but your power.

Same thing can happen now when we're full of joy or confidence or after we've had some mountaintop experience. If you're not careful, if you're not mindful, the cookie monster, the candy-snatcher, or the joy stealer will come, will be lurking about just waiting as you descend from your mountain, or as you drift down off your cloud, or while you are just basking in the afterglow of some high moment, Some thief will be waiting, waiting in the form of a confrontation or situation, just to snatch your joy. Some thief may jump out of the bushes to demand your cookies and your lunch, wanting neither, but wanting to crush your spirit, wanting to take your power, the power that lies in being joy-filled. You see, the strength is in the joy. The joy of the Lord gives you strength. The thief wants to take what makes you strong, your joy. The thief wants to take your cookies, and your lunch, wants to make you cry, feel defeated, lose your power!

The enemy knows that we can be more easily defeated when we are joy-less or when our joy can be taken away too easily. We must not let go of it. We must remember the Joy-giver and hold on with all our might.

One time this girl followed me all the way home, 'cause I said I have to go home first and change my clothes. Silly girl. When my mama was done with her, she left me alone. Sometimes you have to call on somebody bigger to help you hold onto your cookies, and that's ok, too.

O God, help us to hold on to our cookies, to resist the enemy who lurks about looking for an opportunity, and help us to be mindful so that we don't give him that opportunity. Give us, O God, joy that cannot be taken away, joy enough to share and to hold onto at the same time.

For the thief comes to snatch and to take away whatever he can get or whatever you let 'im, but the Good Shepherd comes to give and to give back so that we may live and keep on living!

151

I wish you love
Because that's what we are made of
And what we are made for.
Love is in us
That is how we come to be
From love-making
Not pleasure-seeking,
Though pleasure may be found
But out of love's making
Love-in-the-making
 'Til life comes and comes to be
In us
Through us
In the image of
Made and shaped lovingly
'Til Love in us can Love's own image see.
I wish you love
Today and every day
The feel-ing and ful-filling that only Love can give
And you, out of Love's bounty, can give away.

Kathy Culmer

152

Yes, you can!
Whatever it is that you're needing to,
You can do!
You have a power—THE power—within you
To do whatever it takes to get it done and see you through.
Yes, you can!
You have been here before
Wondering, doubting, waiting,
And you know it's true
Whether to overcome or get it done or try something new
Whatever is facing you
You can and you will do!
This time
And the next one too!

153

Perfectly and Purposefully Made

The backbone's connected to…

Aside from being there to give us dimension and backbone and add to our perspective, I wonder if God didn't give each of us a back to remind us that we were not made to do everything for ourselves. There are just some itches that are beyond our reach. No matter the depth of knowledge or skill, there are some heights that are unattainable by human will alone, some tasks we cannot accomplish on our own, whether because of human design or divine plan without a helping hand. I wonder if it was not by design and plan that we would sometimes have to scratch each other's back, but sometimes that it would take a bigger Hand? Now unto the God who possesses and lovingly dispenses all that we lack and Whose always got our back!

154

Waking or sleeping, O Lord, You fill me with breath and cover me with Your love. You inhabit my thoughts that lead me to my higher self, my better being. You know all about me, the inside and out of me, and still You care for and about me. You give never-ending thought to me. Unbelievable! Having gone before me into this day, into time and even into eternity, to make way for me, You have both made a way for me and prepared the way for me. Countless are Your blessings. Counting my blessings would be like counting my thoughts or raindrops. Never could I catch them all or hold or count or re-count or re-call them all! You never abandon me, whether in the storm or calm, whether on the mountain top or in the valley drop, whether at my best or worst or somewhere in between, seen or unseen, You are with me, Always! Forever Love, Forever Yours!

Thank You. Amen.

155

That thing that seems so hard, maybe even looks impossible to do, that's just God saying, "I've got you. I really won't forsake you." That's just God loving you, trusting you, stretching you, reminding you, "I will be with you," in the little and the bigger stuff, too, to help you do, and see you through, whatever it is you need God to. Trust God and see, Won't He do it! For you!

156

When You're Still Enough to Hear,

Though the world with all its lies would have you think otherwise,
When you draw near enough,
You can hear your Beloved whisper
In your heart, if not your ear,
"You are beautiful, no matter what the world may say.
You are beautiful because I made you that way."

When together in the company of one another and no other
And stillness surrounds
When detractors from peace and quiet are no longer around
And quiet is the only sound
When voices, nor your own thoughts can any longer be heard
In the midst of the silence, you can hear a voice saying, though not with
a word,
"You are loved. With an everlasting love. Born that way. And to stay."

When you leave the noise and the busyness behind
Which too often leave you deaf and blind
And spend some quiet time alone with me, you will once more hear
and see,
"Beloved, you are mine.
You always have been
And will forever be
Throughout eternity."

Be still.
Draw near.
In the quiet.
In the stillness.
In the nearness.
You will hear.
And come to know.
Your Maker.

157

For those who are suffering sickness or sadness, loneliness, loss, or lost-ness, today, those who are grieving, experiencing hopelessness or despair or just don't care today, for those who are hurting in any way, whether the hurt is brand new or hurt you have grown accustomed to. For those who suffer for them and with them or because of them, in your own suffering way. Lord, have mercy on those who are so desperately in need of You, .whether or not they know they do. Touch them with a touch that is unmistakably your touch, in a way that undeniably could come only from You. Reassure them with your love. Restore hope that has been lost or give to them hope that has not yet been found. Fix whatever is in them or in their circumstances that is in need of repair, O God, meet them at the point of their need and let them find You there. Amen.

158

Time Flies. When we race against it, who wins? What's the prize?
At what cost?

In our youth we are so often in a rush,
Hurrying to get there.
Where was that again?
How much did we have to pay
To be on that fast train
Anyway?

Going fast
In a dash
Rushing past
Time and life along the way.
In a hurry
Full of worry
'Til both youth and time have gotten away.

In maturity, we arrive
Glad to still be alive
Living life the best we can
(Living life to the best
With intentionality and zest
Yet)
At a slower pace
No longer in a race
Savoring
Time
And
Life
No longer in a rush to get past
But in every way to make it last.

Kathy Culmer

159

A Lesson from the Growing Plant

We are made in God's image, but we grow into God's likeness.

Plants need sunlight to grow. Plants grow or lean-in towards the sunlight and grow in the sun's direction. In order for them to grow straight, they must be adjusted from time to time so the sun can shine on them from all sides. Where they abide in relationship to the sun affects their growth.

Like the plant, we too need Son-light to grow. It not only helps us to live and grow, but it also helps us to grow and live. And like the plant, to get the full benefit, we will, from time to time, need an adjustment or a repositioning so the Son-light can get to us on all sides, even our insides, and keep us growing in the Son's direction. Our presence with, as well as proximity to the Son can impact our growth, whether sitting at His feet, falling before His face, resting in His love or walking in His light.

Indeed, we are made in God's image, but we grow into God's likeness by leaning towards the Son.

Amen.

160

True love
Loves you through your mess
Never loves you less
Always sees (in you) your best
Desires, above all else, your happiness
When it sees you in distress
Bids you come and take a rest
Cannot help itself, but to express
Maintains its faithfulness
Whether life is at its best or when it puts you to the test
Truelove is nonetheless
It is always there to bless!

161

True light not only lights its own way but lights the way for others. It not only shines its own light but helps others to find theirs, and SHINE.

162

Sometimes you have to say it 'til you mean it, and 'til you believe it too. Sometimes you have to love folks who don't love you, or who don't know how to, and you have to love 'em 'til you mean it and believe it, and they know you do. Sometimes you have to pray it til you mean it, and 'til you believe it too, and that no matter what, God's got you! Sometimes you just gotta keep on, and keep on doing what you do until something changes., or changes in you!

163

Time goes by so fast.
In a moment's time,
It has already passed.
We can only make the most of every moment
We cannot make the moment last.

Once lived, the present moment we were in
Has already become the past.
We look at children and say, "My how they've grown!"
Looking back at our own lives, we ask,
"Where has the time gone?"
Life goes by so quickly, it seems to have flown.
How could we, beforehand, have possibly known?

Unlike money, we cannot work at time to make of it more
But we can work with the time we're given to make of it the most.
As treasured as time is
Its value does not come from our ability to hold on,
But the way it is spent before it's all gone.

Kathy Culmer

164

You know how you pick up a piece of fruit from your fruit bowl, and it's got a bad spot on it, but you don't want to throw it away. So, you don't. Some people might decide to throw it away because of that one spot and they think the fruit is no more good. But, not you. You don't throw it away because you figure it's just that one bad spot and there's still plenty good left in it, that there's juice and ripeness yet to be discovered, and that if you just don't give up on it and keep digging, you'll find it. Besides, you bought the fruit and paid for it and believe that whatever it cost you, it was worth it, and the good that's left of it is worth your effort to cut around it or dig deeper to get to it. So, you don't throw it away, and you keep digging, deeper into the fruit, past the bad part—the rotting part. Sometimes you have to cut deeper than others, but you don't give up, getting closer and closer to the core of the fruit, where the good stuff—the sweetness, the ripeness and the goodness reside. And there, you find your enjoyment and your satisfaction, partly because of its good-ness, but partly because you found what you knew was there all along.

Like fruit in the hands of the one-who-deems-it-worth-it-to-go-deeper-to-get-to-the-good-part, are WE in the hands of the Divine Savourer. Worth digging for. Worth dying for. To get to the best part. And make the goodness last.

Thank You and Amen.

Some days, I can feel the covering of prayers once prayed for me.
Prayer can be like a covering, like spreading a blanket of love over the one prayed for to meet their present needs and later ones too. I know my mother's prayers still do.

Some days, I can feel the covering of prayers once prayed for me,
Reaching to me in the here-and-now from the knees upon which she once knelt,
From love so deeply felt
Prayed with the quiet murmurs of her heart or some agonizing plea
Carried before the Almighty on behalf of me
That all should go well.
Prayers prayed to help me go through
Or to keep me from having to
Or perhaps help me recover when I do
Prayers for a victorious outcome
In whatever I had to come out from
Or to keep me, while coming, so I wouldn't come un-done.

I believe the same is true for the prayers I now pray for my children and others too, that they will keep working on their behalf as long as is needed or until the prayer has succeeded. The effectual, fervent prayers we pray can be like medicine that is still working, healing, and fixing stuff long after the "Amen."

166

Weighing Your Weight

All weight is not equal.
Some weight builds muscle and strength and endurance.
To do what it can, it must be met with resistance.
Some weight weighs you down,
Unevenly distributed, it can make you lose balance
Stunting growth and weakening your stance.
Dead weight it becomes when we hold on for too long
Struggling and striving beneath it
Until the life (in us or the thing) is all gone.
Rendering you unable to advance
Or move on.
Some weight just weighs on you.
You wear/bear it, in spite of, cause you don't know what else to do.
Still, some weight you carry
And must
Because you were meant to.
Yet
Carrying any and all weight, even though we can, is not the best thing to do.
Some, it behooves us to lose.
Wisdom knows the difference.
Still, we must choose.

167

When you come to the mountain, what do you do?
Stare it down, admire its beauty, run from or run to?
Running from might not provide you escape because some mountains will come after you.

Some see the mountain as a big rock that grew.
To some, it may look like an insurmountable obstacle facing you.
Others see it as a new height to climb or aspire to.
Some can't wait to get to the top to see and enjoy the mountain-top view.
But even looking up from the valley can be breath-taking too.

Some see the mountain as a creative challenge that with the right tools they can hew,
Until it becomes something different, more manageable or altogether new.
Some see it as a challenge, a temporary but necessary thing, that with time, determination and perhaps the help of the Mountain-Maker, they can work their way victoriously through.
Some see the mountain as a hurdle to overcome on the way to a breakthrough.
Others may glory in this masterpiece of nature whose beauty and vastness to take in is beyond your purview.

Then, there are some who see the mountain as the end of the journey, sad but true,
A stopping point, a thing to give into,
A sign to turn around and go home because there's nothing else you can do.

Some mountains elevate, while others humble you.
Whatever, in the face of the mountain, you can or cannot do
You can always enlist the help of the Mountain Maker
To carry you,
Over, around, or through,

Or perhaps from the valley or plain where you stand, lift your eyes towards the hills so that even from a distance or a depth you can enjoy and appreciate the awesome panoramic view.

Kathy Culmer

168

Some sip slowly
and deliberately
so they can savor and let none go to waste.
Some gulp in haste
barely getting a taste.
Therefore,
Drink deeply of life
And partake often of its pleasures.
For though its length and breadth cannot be measured
Time well-spent with loved ones
Will above all else be treasured.

May your treasure chest grow daily.

Kathy Culmer

169

We live in a technology-driven world, full of devices to help meet our needs or satisfy some desire. We rely on these devices to give us directions, manage our schedules, and keep us connected. From the first click of the morning, however, and with each subsequent click or stroke, their energy supply is being depleted. They consistently need recharging to function as designed.

To keep them operational, we have chargers in our homes, our cars, in our pockets or purses. We become frantic and frustrated when one can't be found, or when the battery is running low. We fear losing power.

Prayer is like those chargers. It allows us immediate access to God, our ultimate power source. Prayer keeps us charged and connected. It gives us power to keep running.

Pray. Without ceasing. It will help you avoid a power outage.

Amen.

170

"Jesus told them. 'I tell you the truth, if you
had faith even as small as a mustard seed,'"
Matt. 17:20

What if faith is really like that mustard seed, whose size had no bearing on what grew out of it, once it was planted in the ground, but having been released, grew into a tree that provided refuge and a resting place for the birds of the air? What if the size of our faith doesn't determine the return on it, like we may have thought, 'cause we've grown accustomed to thinking that more and bigger is always better? But, what if the size doesn't matter as much as the use or the working of it, the letting go of it to see what will grow when we do?

After all, the seed didn't grow until the farmer put it in the ground, and like every other seed that is planted, stuff took place that couldn't be seen, and that the planter had nothing to do with. Some mystery happened that made more of it coming out of the ground than what it was going into the ground. What if faith is like that?

What if faith is really our willingness to keep putting it out there, not knowing what it will look like when it comes out of the ground, but doing it any way so the unseen and the stuff we have nothing to do with can happen, putting whatever amount we've got out there, not to make more of it so much as to grow bolder and more confident in our letting go of it? What if God isn't asking, expecting or even caring whether we have a lot or a little faith, as much as God is caring that we put the faith we have out there where something can grow from it? What if, in the case of our faith, size really doesn't matter, 'cause faith isn't really about us and what we can do anyway? What if our prayers for more faith became, instead, Lord, here's the faith I've got, whatever the size of my faith, let it not be a hindrance to growth, not to mine or anybody else's or to whatever might grow from it. Let mine be a faith that allows something to grow out of it, so it can produce something, so that maybe the birds of the air can find rest in its branches, and I in its shade.

Kathy Culmer

171

When handing me my order, the lady at McDonald's said, "Here you go, Beautiful." I don't know what my face was saying before, but hearing her say this, it beamed a big thank you of a smile and the words to go with it. I said some other words of appreciation to the lady before I drove away, but even as I did, she called out to me to say, "Hey, don't forget to share that beautiful smile with someone else today." Needless to say, she made my day or a pretty big impression on me anyway, reminding me once more of how easy it is to brighten someone else's day, when we're willing to take even a small portion of the best in us we have to offer and give it away.

172

"My life is but a breath."
Job 7:7

As I live and breathe...
Breathing is a moment-by-moment reminder of our dependence on a source outside ourselves, of our dependence on God for the next breath to live. It is the first thing we check for when life begins and when it ends. Breath cannot be stored or amassed; it must be used as it is received. Breath was not meant to be held onto but to keep life flowing in and out of you.

It must be lived. As. It. Is. Breathed.

Even if we hold our breath, it does not give us extra. Because it is such a necessary thing, an automatic thing, a frequent occurrence, we take it for granted as though it will always be there. It is so routine that we hardly think of it unless something gets in the way and hinders our airflow. Moment-by-moment, breath-by-breath we must rely upon the Eternal Source of all breath and life to live. Breathing on our own, like living on our own, cannot be done only on our own. Just thinking and giving thanks...as I live and breathe. Amen.

Kathy Culmer

173

Judgment is a tricky thing. It casts a wide net, often ensnaring the one who cast it. When we are heaping coals of condemnation on others, we must take care that we are not constructing pyres for ourselves. When we start passing judgment, we better check where and how we stand, because you never know when you pass it, where it might land, and whether the solid ground on which you thought you stood might turn out to be sinking sand.

Kathy Culmer

174

Lord, there is no one, no none, like You! You have been our deliverer and sustainer throughout the seasons of our lives. You have ordained and framed our days and fit us for them, and them for us. You have never withheld Your hand of mercy nor failed to extend Your hand of grace. You have kept us, and kept us from, and kept watch, and kept us keeping on. You have guided us to, and guided us through, and guided us well beyond. Thank You, Lord! You have been our deliverer and sustainer throughout the seasons of our lives, You are still,   And, you always will. Lord, there is no one, no none, like You!

Amen!

175

Have you ever missed a blessing because it didn't look like you thought it would? Or because you were so focused on the bad that happened you couldn't see the good? Sight can be deceiving although it's what lets us see. Looking and seeing work differently. You can look and look and never find. With eyes wide open you can still be blind. Looking is based on images you see in your mind. Seeing discerns the soul-deep truth of what you find.

"What did you go out to see," Jesus asked those who questioned who He was. Often what we see is the result of what we go looking for or how we look at what we find.

176

You are our Way-maker, O Lord! When doubt casts its shadow and tears cloud our view, when despair gets in the way and we temporarily lose sight of You, when pain wracks our bodies or being, rendering us powerless to do, You, O Lord, always come through, making a way out of no way, fixing the old way, or if You have to, making it all new. We thank You, O Lord, for giving us a way and being our way as only You can do, and for the grace to see our way and make it through.

Help me to see the way today, O Lord, Help me to see my way, Your way, and to walk in it.

Amen!

177

Suffering through to Give Birth to Something New

The darkest part of night comes just before the morning light.

Giving birth is both a glorious and a painful process. In all its pain and glory, it is a process necessary to facilitate new life. The bearer of new life (the bearer of the unborn) must almost always endure some pain, some discomfort, some stretching in order to accommodate new life, whether to produce new life or to make a way for it to be born. And, while he or she must suffer for the sake of the yet unborn, they do so with the anticipation of the joy and reward that will follow.

The caterpillar must press through its cocoon to become a butterfly. Nymphs must work their way through well-worn skin to become dragonflies. Mothers, no matter their genus, must endure labor pains; they must push and press simultaneously to bring forth their young. Dreamers must do battle with dream stealers to see the dream through its necessary gestation, in order to make realities of imagined possibilities. In these cases, suffering through the pain and the hard parts for a prescribed period of time are necessary until something new can come into being.

When the time comes to finally give birth, whether to new life or to a new thing in us, the labor pains will intensify and the struggle and pain may seem too much for us to bear, alone. In spite of the temptation to give up, however, we are compelled to push on through the pain as the pain pushes new life through us.

Suffering will come, of this we can be sure, but God will not leave us alone our suffering to endure, until suffering has made way for something new or until it has made something new of you. It is how we respond to our suffering that lets us our true selves see, and it is what we allow our suffering to bring out of us that helps us become the selves we were meant to be.

Help us, O God, to press through the times, the circumstances, the darkness, the unbearable, whatever the birth canal through which we must pass to get through life or to get to the new life that awaits us. Give us grace and strength to push and keep on pushing until we have made it through, and in all our circumstances give us hope to never give up on You.

I press on, forgetting what is behind and straining toward what is ahead, I press on toward the goal, to win the prize!

178

No matter how dry on the surface they may look to you, you never know what storm somebody has just come through, how torrential the rain, how mighty the wind they had to battle during the storm they were in, whether without or within. Perhaps the best thing any of us could do would be to love everybody as we would if we knew what or if they were going through. You never know. Your love, kindness, encouraging word or even smile, might just help them to. 'Cause one thing we can count on for true, there's always a storm coming whether for somebody else or you.

Kathy Culmer

179

God speaks. All around and everywhere. Seeking an ear that will hear and heed, a heart that will receive and believe, God speaks indeed.

God speaks. All round and about. Like wind—sometimes in a whisper, sometimes with a shout, through our circumstances and His Word, God speaks out. Sometimes in silence, with sound or without, God speaks, without a doubt.

God speaks. All around us, the heavens declare God's glory; the skies proclaim God's handiwork! What we have seen and heard give voice to God's Word. God speaks to our yearning and hears our praise, when our voices we raise, and receives our heartfelt offerings made in a myriad of ways.

God speaks. All around and everywhere. With purpose and intent—deep to deep—God speaks, our lives to live and souls to keep.

O God, help us to be aware and be still. Let Your speech draw us near. Help us to discern Your voice and Your will. Incline our hearts and ears to listen and hear.

Amen.

180

"But as for me, I watch in hope for the Lord"
Micah 7:7

God is able.
But how could we know?
Until we've had some dreaded journey to take, that we thought we'd never make, and God enabled us to, never letting go.

God is able.
But how could we know?
Until we've found ourselves in some desolate valley, with no way out in sight and God fed us with the experience, nourished us with His love and there helped us grow.

God is able.
But how could we know?
Until the weight of debt or guilt or sin has us bent so low we can't see how to move or move on and God reminds us, in some indisputable way, "I've already paid that debt for you, and you no longer owe."

God is able.
But how could we know?
Until God has led us to some mountain top
Or kept us while in some valley below
Whether on the heights or in the depths
God's glory there to show.

God is able.
But how could we know?
Trust. And. Live.
Life's encounters will teach us so
With countless evidence to show
So without a doubt
When we come out
We will know
And in that knowledge grow.

Kathy Culmer

God is able.
This I know to be true
Whatever in life you come to
Regardless of what you can or cannot
On your own do
God's got you.
God is able.
And God will see you through!

Kathy Culmer

181

Up too soon
Still see the moon
Or is it just darkness that you see
Even though it's noon?
Don't worry
Daylight is coming
Even if on delay
Hold on
Son/sunshine is on the way.
Hope you catch a ray or two
And that the Son/sun will get to you.

182

How to know we can't beat God's giving—

Count up every breath you've taken since birth and multiply it times its worth, not to mention every minute and whatever good was in it, knowing too that it was God who sent it. Now, breathe out and back in, and every time you do, there goes God giving once again.

How to know we can't beat God giving
Just keep living.
No way could we repay or ever give that much away.

Kathy Culmer

183

"Can any of you by worrying add a single hour to your span of life?"
Luke 12:25

When my daughter comes home to visit, she brings few toiletries with her. She knows that certain essentials will already be available to her for her use, her comfort and convenience, so, she only brings the "extra stuff." This lightens her load, takes up less room in her bags, and if she is traveling by air, can cost her less in checked bags. Her goal is to travel as unencumbered as she can.

Worry is like those too-heavy bags, filled with non-essential stuff, stuff that will weight us down and cost us more, whether in money or anxiety. It is of no benefit to us, only a hindrance. Worry is like dead weight, and trying to carry that load will either exhaust us or leave us feeling lifeless. I pack too heavy, often carrying far more clothes than I ever wear, getting frustrated from trying to get the stuffed-too-tightly bag closed, and worrying whether I'll have to pay additional baggage fees. Trust enables us to leave the overload out of our travel bags, avoid additional baggage fees and rest assured that every provision will be made for our use, our comfort and well-being, as by the loving parent who welcomes us home.

184

Persistence is the seed that didn't quit until it became a tree. It is the single drop of water that didn't stop until it reached the sea. Persistence is all those steps you take to reach your mountain tops and come down to earth again before your stepping stops. It is the thought that wouldn't let go of you until it became your dream-come-true, and kept on until it had convinced others that theirs could too! Persistence is the can-do and the will-to-do that kept on and kept on doing, until it was all done.

185

"Cast your cares on God, because God cares for you."
1 Peter 5:7

God can. And God will.
You know that thing you've been trying so hard and so long to do, but no matter what, you can't seem to.
God can. And God will.

You know that problem you've been seeking a solution to, been wrestling with day and night trying to figure out but still don't know what to do.
God can. And God will.

You know that weight you've been carrying since it was just a little ol' something you thought you could handle until that something grew, into something so heavy it feels it might break your back in two, or break you, that thing that you can no longer handle on your own, or alone, because it's just too much for you.
God can. And God will.

Whatever it is you're going through where you find the going hard to do or wonder if you'll ever make it through,
Whatever thing it is you're facing that seems impossible to you,
You can know, without a doubt, because it's true,
God's got your solution, and God's got you!
God can. And God will.

186

Something to chew on, spit out, or rinse your thoughts off with,
If you don't like the direction your life is taking you, stop being taken and take another way. But first, make sure you consult a good map and that you are following a trustworthy guide. There is an infallible navigation system, the ultimate GPS (God's Positioning System), that you might consult each day Who will give you sound directions and help you find your way, even when you stray.

Let Love Live
(Let it LIve in me and LOve out of me.)

Let love live in me
Let it live and breathe in and out of me.
For some it comes more easily
Not so for me.
Come
Love
Fill
Me
Go deep in me
To the very depths of me
My soul to keep
From heart, to start
Then caressing, mending, shaping,
Taking hold of
Every part
Of me
To make the best and the most of me.

Let love live in me
Breathing in and out of me
Filling and spilling over in and out of me
All around and round about me
Delighting me and in me
Drawing me
Binding
And intertwining
With love above
Three-in-One
One with me
Me in unity with humanity
Love-bound but without boundary
From earth below to eternity.

Kathy Culmer

Let Love Live
Let it LIve in me and LOve out of me.
That's when love can be all that it was meant to be.

Kathy Culmer

188

O Lord, give us this day, our daily bread. May it add strength to our bodies and provide nourishment to our souls. Give us an appetite for this bread and let us receive it with thanksgiving. Sometimes our cravings are for bread that will not fill us or sustain us or that may result in excess weight. Help us, O God, in our bread-cravings and our inclinations to seek bread elsewhere. Curb our appetites for that which will bloat us, that which will not sustain us, or that which never really fills us, though for a while it may cause us to feel full. Cultivate our taste for bread that will truly satisfy our hunger and fulfill our needs, and let us graciously receive it, savor it, and share generously with others.

Thank you and Amen.

Kathy Culmer

189

Sound Bites
They are being served up
The whole day through
But what are they really supposed to do
Give you a taste
Or take a bite out of you?

Sound bites are like the food we eat on the run, too often tasteless, not easily digested, occasionally causes bloating and can leave you with heartburn. They are served in portions that make them easy to swallow without chewing. They can make you full or feel full, but most often do not fill you. And while they come in appetizer-sized portions, they are not the same. The appetizer is to make us want more, the sound bite is meant to convince us we have had enough. Chewing can help us discern the taste and swallowing without first doing so will certainly make waste. Sometimes it takes a knife and fork to know.

Help us with our consumption, O God. Help us to have discerning palates and the resolve to make healthier choices for the nourishment of our bodies, our minds and our souls. Help us to digest only those things that will serve us well and that will help us serve you well. And please don't let anything we consume stick that will in any way make us sick. Amen.

190

And God said, 'Let there be, " And it was so!
Wonder if God spoke love into life at the same time God spoke life into being? Did love or life come first or simultaneously? Did God come to love, or was love there in the beginning? New life is born of love. Do we come to life knowing love, and can life somehow cause us to forget? Does one come to love by living, or does one come to live by loving? New life is born of love, so too eternal life! God is. Love. And life. Concurrently. Eternally.
To You, O God who has made all that is in creation
For Your good pleasure and for our use and recreation
Let us not defy Your trust
But honor and care for all You've entrusted to us
Incline us to love and to do
All in creation
That You have made us and willed us to
With hearts and minds to ever seek and never cease to follow You.

Amen

191

Excess Weight

Who wants to carry extra weight around? Weight is heavy enough, without carrying extra.

Trust takes the weight off you. It assures you that what needs to be done will be done, with or without you. It's not about you or dependent on you, or about what you can or cannot do. There is a power greater than you. When you let worry go, it will let go of you. Perhaps not without a fight, but even then, Trust will win the fight for you. When you really let go and trust, that's what Trust will do. Trust takes the weight off you and puts it in the hands of the One who can best carry it for you.

192

One step at a time
Grace to find and
Strength to climb
Out of the hole/hold
That seeks to hinder and confine
In body, circumstance or mind.
On step at a time
Grace to find and
Strength to climb
(Sometimes even the next step seems too great an incline.)
Seeing or not the next step
Or following as faith would lead me in the blind.
One grace-filled step at a time
Help me to take or climb
'Til I have reached the peace, the promise, the higher ground intended
to be mine.

Kathy Culmer

193

Giving to Get Full

We can sometimes feel empty not because of what we don't have, but because of what we don't give, not because of what we have not ourselves received but because of what we have not given to others. When a person sees the glass as being half empty instead of half full, that person is considered to be a pessimist, some say, but even when we see the glass as half-empty it does not mean we see it the same way. Every half-empty or even empty glass is not necessarily that way because of what wasn't poured into it, but sometimes it is because of what has already been poured out of it. In such cases, the glass could be seen not as being empty, but as no longer full, not because it never was, but because Its contents have been consumed, used to quench someone's thirst. When feeling empty, perhaps we should check the level of our giving, whether or not we have given enough or too little, and if we are empty because of our giving, we may only need a re-filling.

194

Lord, I love it when You say, dream bigger, breathe deeper, go further and then You make it happen! I love how You can take what looks like an ending and make it a new beginning, how You turn a door that looks like it's closing into a swinging door that opens up wide to all sorts of new possibilities on the other side! I love it when You turn despair around into hope, when You take something old and make it brand new, when it looks like it's all over and You say, "Not yet, I'm not through!" Lord, I love how You do You, all by Yourself! I love how you love!

195

Losing Well

I wonder if sometimes and, in some ways, folks who know how to lose well don't get along better than folks who just know how to win. By this, I am in no way suggesting that we play to lose or strive to be unsuccessful, but that perhaps we could look more readily for ways to maximize our losses/failures/disappointments and be less inclined to allow them to defeat us or to get to us.

With the heavy emphasis our world places on winning and winning at all cost, and with the inevitability of not taking top prize every time, I just wonder if we could do a better job of teaching our children how to lose, how to fail so they'll know how to respond when things just don't turn out the way they were hoping, just in case, if we shouldn't do a better job of teaching them that loss is not synonymous with failure and only becomes failure when we let it stop there, and do a better job of teaching them that most losses come with opportunity, and that losing should not stop us but propel us, by reminding us that we are not yet all we can be, but that if we keep trying we certainly will be.

196

"As the clay is in the potter's hand, so are you in my hand."
Jeremiah 18:6

Ernest is a great artist! He would come to church, sit in the back and with pen in hand create flawless drawings of the people and sights around him. He would use ink and not pencil to make his drawings, which was always amazing to me. I couldn't imagine drawing anything without an eraser. Even with a simple drawing, I expect to make some mistakes and would then need an eraser to try and wipe them away (but that's a story for another day). I'm not an artist though. At least not that kind.

When the artist makes a mistake or goes outside the line, he takes it and works it into the design. He does not use an eraser to erase the flaws away, he lets them stay and uses them in some way. He keeps on working his pen to work any mistakes or extraneous marks in to make them blend, so they are picture-perfect in the end. He skillfully works them in so well that by the time the drawing is finished, the eye cannot tell what from the beginning was intended and what has been amended. That's what an artist will do—keep working it all in—the good with the bad until the picture is perfect and the work is all through.

Like great works of art on the canvas of the Designer of Creation are we —to perfection being designed—as conceived in God's own mind; throughout a lifetime, into God's glory and likeness are we, in-the-making and in the end to see.

197

"For we are God's masterpiece."
Ephesians 2:10 (NLT)

Perfectly made, imperfections and all, an Artist's rendering, not yet in full view. While it does not yet appear what we shall be, though purposed in eternity, when You, O Lord, are all through, your work complete in us, we will be and all will see, a masterpiece revealing the likeness of You, by divine design only later to reflect both hand and face of the Artist and Creator. How great are your works, O Lord!

Thank You and Amen!

198

Time is expendable.

Make sure you spend it well before it's fully spent.
Though you never can re-pay it, they say that time is lent.
And since it's non-refundable, be sure and spend it for what it's meant.
Above all, enjoy your spending of the time you're given and to its full
extent.

Because in no time you'll have spent it all and wonder where it all went.

199

Seeds that the earth does not receive simply fall on dry ground. They cannot grow. They cannot become. Same is true for life's lessons delivered to us by seeds of experience. Unless we open ourselves to receiving these seeds, they lie dormant on trails not taken or dry up into nothingness on pathways of forgetfulness. They can never get inside and do the work they came to do, take root in us, grow us or produce their intended fruit.

200

Keep Flying

My mother's roommate in the nursing home where she spent the last 3 years of her life was Mrs. Hite. Under the most difficult of circumstances, Mrs. Hite was a gift.

Whenever I would greet Mrs. Hite and ask her how she was doing, her standard answer was, "Kicking high, fluttering but can't fly." That always made me smile, because Mrs. Hite could neither kick nor fly. She had no legs.

Her response was so opposite to her circumstances. She, her physical self, at least, was confined to a wheelchair. She couldn't go anywhere, not too far anyway, unless somebody took her there. Yet, her response had to do with rising up on air.

Her words did lift, in a sense, because they brought that smile, but being able to think such a thought and say it may have kept her lifted as well.

That would be Mrs. Hite's response most days, except on those when she was unable to get out of bed or was too weary to speak because of the effects of the diabetes that had robbed her of her legs. But on those days when she had breath and strength to say the words, her response to the question, "How're you doing today, Mrs. Hite, was, with a smile, "Oh, I'm kicking high, fluttering but can't fly." Right up until the time she got her wings.

Those who wait, who have hope in the Almighty, shall get wings, and fly. Is. 40:31

Kathy Culmer

201

"Even if all others abandon me, the LORD will hold me close."
Psalm 27:10, NLT/IMOW

Sometimes God takes us in His arms so He can hold us up.
Sometimes God takes us in His arms so He can hold us close.
Sometimes God takes us in His arms so He can hold us close to one another.
Sometimes God takes us in His arms so we can know that we are being held.

202

Who Are You?

Who are you?
For true?
What makes you you?
Is it who you are
Or what you do?
Is it how you see
Or are seen
Or the unseen
That shows the true you?

Are you yet you
Or still growing into?

What does the packaging have to do
With you?
Are you you because of the skin you're in
Or what lies within?
If the outside were not there, who would you be then?
What if we lay all aside,
Leaving nothing to hide
What would be left to show?
Unless and until we are willing to let the outside go
No one will ever truly know.

203

Word Power

Words have power.
Misspoken words drift like grit in the air.
Once released, they could end up pretty much anywhere,
Wreaking all sorts of havoc, intended or not, of which you're unaware.
You can never retrieve and seldom repair
The damage words do when you carelessly put them out there.
Yes, words can do all that and much more, If you don't take care.

204

Fix the Fit

We like our clothes to fit, to be comfortable and to look good on us. And while we don't want to go around all the time feeling the discomfort of clothes that fit too tightly around our expanding bulge, sometimes we may need to feel a pinch here or a squeeze there to remind us of our indiscretions and overindulgences, to alert us of areas we need to pay some attention to, to prompt us to do what we need to do to get ourselves back in shape again, so we don't get too comfortable where we are and want to stay there, whether that means changing sizes or reducing the bulge.

205

Sometimes I wonder if God doesn't listen in on some of our intense discussions, debates, and arguments on matters of faith and scratch a cloud in wonderment, smile a rainbow with pleasure or maybe even spit a shooting star in sheer delight, then say something like, "My beloveds! They still don't get me. But they're trying. And desiring. And I can work with that." Or something like that.

Kathy Culmer

206

Remembering…

One day when my mother was well into the throes of dementia, sometimes unable to call my name or distinguish me from her mother (yet recognizing me as a loving presence nonetheless), I asked her, "Mur, do you love Jesus?" With little or no hesitation, she answered, "Yes." I then asked her why. She answered, "Because He first loved me." That is the kind of unwavering faith and assurance that I long to have—the kind that in spite of my ability to reason or remember, that even when I am no longer knowing, I can still know.

Kathy Culmer

207

Walking in the Dark

Walking gives us good exercise.
Even when we have to do it in the dark.
My first job was at Kentucky Fried Chicken in Griffin, Georgia. I was excited to have that job even though I felt like I gained weight just smelling the chicken. Sometimes I would have to work until it got dark, and when I did my mother and my Aunt Mae would come and meet me and walk me home. We didn't have a car, so I did lots of walking. Ordinarily, I enjoyed walking and didn't mind at all, but not by myself at night. I especially enjoyed walking along with my mama and Aunt Mae, hearing their laughter and listening to them talk about whatever. They were good company, and they kept me from having to walk alone. Being with them made me less aware of the darkness and seemed to make the time pass more quickly. I felt safe with them.

The night was there. The darkness was there. It was inevitable. Darkness is. And, it can sometimes be scary. Especially when traveling alone.

Nighttime is much more navigable and far less intimidating when you do not have to walk in it alone and when you have someone to walk it with you who knows the way. I was comforted knowing I had someone, my mama and my Aunt Mae, to walk with me in the dark until I was safely home. I was awfully grateful back then that I had someone to rely on to walk with me through the dark. I am grateful today that I still do. "When you go through, I will be with you," says the Lord. (Is. 43:2)

Thanks be to God! Amen.

208

God has no doubt about you!
Even when you do.
God knows you for true
And knows you through and through.
What it takes a lifetime to uncover and for each of us ourselves to
discover,
God already knew
From the first thought of you!

209

"Remember how the Lord your God fed you all the way in the wilderness these forty years, to humble and test you in order to know what was in your heart, He humbled you, causing you to hunger and then feeding you with manna."
(Deut. 8:2-3)

I wonder if God didn't make us to get hungry as a reminder to us to keep feeding ourselves with that which is necessary to sustain life. With having fast food places, frozen food sections, and home delivery services so readily available to us, we hardly have the chance to hunger any more. Many have never known real hunger since at its first pangs, we grab the first thing we can put our hands on to quiet our hunger so no one will hear.

Sometimes, though, we need to get hungry and to get hungry enough to realize what it is we hunger for, or better yet, what it is that will fill us and then go searching for it until we find it. Our parents and grandparents abided by the principle, "When you get hungry enough, you'll eat," and in many cases, we did. Now, we eat for taste and convenience more often than we do to feed our hunger, feeding ourselves with stuff that can fatten us but not fill us.

Heaven's food requires deep hunger and an acquired taste before we can taste and see and receive.

210

We are made
And being made in God's image
Yet ever being and becoming as God would have us be
Shaped and formed and fashioned into God's likeness
More and more of God in us to see
It does not yet appear what we shall be
But when and then, our Maker's face to see
Fearfully
Wonderfully
Made and made perfectly
Being and becoming perfected
Daily
As more and more God shapes and takes shape in me
Molding, making us to be what we cannot yet
But know that we shall someday see
That which God has known since before we ever came to be
More and more and more of God in me
"Til God in me should Be
And God's own self God should see
Planned and purposed so to be
Since time before, and throughout all eternity
Amen.

Kathy Culmer

211

When We Can No Longer Hear the Song or Remember the Words, But
Need to Sing

My mother couldn't sing a tune, but every now and again, she would
belt out a song, and when she did,
Whether in celebration or sorrow,
It let me know that everything was all right,
Or was gonna be so.

Sometimes we just gotta sing!
Sometimes 'cause we just want to, sometimes 'cause we have to,
Sometimes 'cause the song won't keep silent, and sometimes 'cause it
gives us the breath or beat we need to make it through. Sometimes,
with moans and groans and words untold but fully comprehended by
the soul.

How can we sing the Lord's Song when our breath keeps getting taken
away?
God is our refuge and strength.
In times like these,
A very present help in trouble.
We sing to remember.
NOW, MORE THAN EVER, WE MUST!

Therefore we will not fear.
We must SING,
When muzzled by mayhem
We must SING,
When stifled by tears and crippled by fears
We must SING,
When the song gets caught in our throats
We must SING,
When we can no longer hear ourselves singing
Or nobody else will sing along
We must SING
And KEEP ON singing.

Kathy Culmer

212

The problem with using labels is that they can only tell a partial truth. They simply don't have enough words in them to relay what the whole truth has to say. To label me by color or gender may celebrate or hinder, but either only represents one part of me. The rest of me and the best of me is the part that you can't see. Labels are used to keep people in their place and out of our way, to hold one another at bay. While labels may be useful to organize and categorize, misuse of them can polarize and traumatize, partial truth in disguise trying to sell themselves off as the whole truth to the unwise, or the non-discerning or whoever buys or buys into the lies, that labels can sometimes tell. We use labels because they are handy and quick and don't take much breath or time, they don't require much of us, and, well, because we like packaging that sells, quick and in a hurry, whether our possessions, or our views, even though a partial view, never mind the fact that what sells tells people what not to buy too.

213

Prayer is like the planting of seeds and letting them go (trusting). Praise is like the watering and tending we do to help them (and us) grow, to let our gratitude show and the true Gardener know.

When you plant a seed, you let it go. You water it and tend it as best you can, but the seed can't grow while still in hand. You must let go. You cannot watch or make it grow. You trust what you cannot see. Its growth begins in the earth below. The next time you see it, it is no longer the seed you put in the ground, but what the seed has grown into, after it has come through the earth into which it was sown.

Not unlike prayer. You pray the prayer, and you water it with trust. In confidence, you wait for fruit. To reap a harvest, we must. Some of us, for lack of trust, sometimes, nearly dig up the seed that we'd planted with prayer. But what we don't know or often enough remember is that we cannot make the seed grow, neither with worry nor with woe. We can only let it go.

May the seeds of your longing take root, and may you have the peace of knowing as they are growing and becoming fruit. Amen.

Kathy Culmer

214

Being is not always an easy thing. Sometimes it is easier to do than to be. If we are not mindful, our doing can muddle our being, So that the me that I and others see, is not the true me, but a facsimile.

"Be" is at the beginning of believing, becoming, belonging.

Could this mean that we must first "be" before we can do any of these three, authentically?

When babies are young, you buy some things to fit them, and some things you buy for them to grow into. Same thing for you is true. Not with what you wear but with the things in life that face you. Some things that you face, perfectly suit you and you can, with minimal effort or hardship do. Others, at first, are too big for you. You have to do some growing before they fit you. That may, in fact, be the reason they are there for you: to give you something to grow into or something to grow you.

215

What's Your Smell

One of our daughters was home for the weekend, and when I walked into the bathroom the morning she left, I smelled her cologne, a pleasant reminder that she had been there. It made me smile, remembering. When my granddaughter leaves after a visit, it's the same thing, I walk into the room where she got dressed for school, and I smell her smell, and I smile. When another daughter was buying our grandson "big guys'" deodorant, I could smell him long after he was no longer there. He liked the smell too, and that's no doubt the reason his smell lasted so long after he was gone.

You can tell a lot about a person from the smell they leave behind. When I'm out walking sometimes, I'll walk past people or walk into a space where they have already come and gone and smell the remnant of their having been there. It might be a fresh out of the dryer smell, or cologne (yeah, some people have the smell during their morning walk or run, whether the application was made that morning or the night before I don't know), and then of course sometimes there is the smell of sweat. Whatever the smell, it tells me something about the wearer/bearer. And then there are some passers-by who leave no smell, leaving nothing about them to tell.

That got me thinking about my own, what fragrance I want to leave behind when I'm gone. What fragrance do I leave behind when I've been somewhere? What fragrance do I want to leave? Would anyone want to come along behind me? Would I? What sweetness was in the air while I was there? Scripture says, God uses us "to spread the knowledge of Christ everywhere, like a sweet perfume. Our lives are a Christ-like fragrance rising up to God" (2 Cor. 2:14-15).

Smell conjures up stuff. Good or bad, the nose knows. Help us, O God, to leave the fragrance of You behind wherever we go this day, a fragrance pleasing to You and to those who meet us along the way. Thank You and Amen.

Kathy Culmer

216

"Do the things that show you really have changed your hearts and lives."
Matthew 3:8 (NCV)

Why God Requires Repentance and Not Just an Apology

On a recent visit to a country outside the U.S., my daughter was trying to get to a location she had planned to visit. Unfamiliar with the language and the landscape, she found it difficult to find her way there without assistance. Even with a map in her hand, she walked for hours going the wrong way. Only when she found someone who knew the way, did she discover that she had for much of the day been going in the wrong direction. Only by turning around and changing her direction could she reach her desired destination. Had she never stopped for directions or followed them when she received them, she could have continued along her way, going the wrong way.

Yeah, if you don't ever stop and turn around on the road you're traveling, you'll just keep on going the way you're going, even though you may stop here and there to acknowledge you're going the wrong way.

Do those things to show you have turned around. Mt. 3:8

[An apology is the acknowledgement, the oops in recognition that you're going the wrong way. Repentance is turning around and going the right way.]

217

When silent tears fall from dry eyes
When the water has all fallen from your eye and you have none left to
cry,
With aches and sighs
And stifled cries
Pain so deep it has lost its sound
Too much the cost.
Words no longer to be found_
Grief almost too heavy to bear, take it to the Lord in prayer, Help me
Lord to live and love and care, and not to give in to despair
Even when my breath is short and I must gasp for air,
Even when too much crying and dying and sighing have caused my
ducts to run too dry, to cry, this time and the next, and my heart to
bleed my eyes dry.
Most merciful, God,
Compassionate One,
What once flowed from Heartbreak and Hope,
Please restore
The sound to my tears
Their cleansing, healing power once more.

Amen.

Kathy Culmer

218

Bad Attitude Be Gone, Leave me Alone!

When that bad attitude comes creeping your way,
Resist and send it away.
You don't have to let it stay;
All you have to do is say (and mean it),
"Oh no, I'm not letting you in my space today;
In fact, you'll be getting no more play,
Today or any other day
No way!
I know you've come knocking here lots of times before
And grown accustomed to me, every time, opening the door
I don't know what on earth I let you in for,
But no more!
I am sick of you, for sure!
In the past, I haven't had the strength to resist or the will to ignore,
But, I've got a new attitude that's gonna help me wage this war,
And you, Bad Attitude, will not be having your way with me any more!"

Kathy Culmer

219

I Love to Dance

But don't do it much anymore. Whether it's lifestyle or age, I don't often find myself on the dance floor. Then, when I do go to an event where dancing's going on, too often I sit there and say, "I'll sit this one out, 'cause that's not my song," and let my chance to dance get away. But dancing is as much about attitude as it is a thing to do. When you're "feeling it," you don't have to wait for the right song to dance to, any time and any place will do, 'cause the music you're dancing to will be in your head and heart and the dance in you.

Lord, help me to keep on dancing even when I can no longer hear my song, or when the notes come out wrong, or when I have to dance the dance alone. Even when I can no longer hear the music, please help me to keep moving along, until the old one returns or until You give me a new song.

Thank You and Amen.

Kathy Culmer

220

For the sick and tired who are sick and tired of being that way

Healing requires more of us than simply acknowledging our aches and pains and discomforts, or expressing our dislike for the prescribed medication for what ails us, because we do not like its taste or its effect on us or because it costs too much. Neither does healing come by laying blame on the thing that's making us sick. Rarely, if ever, does our healing come about from complaining or wallowing in the dread of our circumstances. Such responses and reactions alone are certain to leave us in our infirmity. Healing requires something of us. We must take the medicine in order for it to do us any good. Even when the Great Healer healed, the healing did not come by idleness.

"Take up your mat and walk."
"Wipe the spittle from your eyes."
"Lazarus, come forth."

If all we do is sit by the pool and watch as others emerge from the healing waters, then we will languish in our misery, a misery to which we have grown too accustomed or too comfortable, and we will ultimately remain cripples by the pool. We are inevitably confronted with the question, "Do you want to be healed?" To answer in the affirmative is our starting place. We must then move. If it is injustice that makes you sick, take a stand; right every wrong you can. If it is hatred that you hate, love all you can. If it is poverty that nauseates you, then give whatever it is you can muster to give, and inspire others to do the same. If it is the condition of the world that grieves you, make things better in the part of it that you inhabit. Do something. Even if you must belly crawl until you can once again walk upright.

221

There is a distant shore
I've never seen before
What's there I do not know, but yearn to more and more
Faith calls me to explore
A call I'm tempted to ignore, I have before
Fear offers a detour
Through an all-too-familiar door
Too many times it's been the door I chose to go for
But, I'll never know for sure
What treasures are in store
Unless I let trust take me where I've never gone before.

Kathy Culmer

222

You, O God, are the One who sees. You see what we hide and what we show. You see the truth of our lives that we have forgotten or that we deny, that we refuse to see or don't yet know, and You forgive us anyhow, love us anyhow, bless us anyhow! You, O God, are the One who knows, all and all about us, and You patiently and lovingly allow us a lifetime to discover the self You had already known and had always loved. For Your eyes, O God, that always keep watch, for your loving care all the time and everywhere, and for Your love that refuses to let us fall or stay fallen, with thanksgiving we pray.

Amen.

223

You know how excited young children can get at birthday parties when it's time to open presents. They get excited about opening their own presents, of course, but they also get excited about having their presents opened by the child whose birthday is being celebrated. They want their presents, that special something they have brought to the person being celebrated, to be opened first. They are eager for that person to hurry up and see what's inside, to see what they brought for you, what has been purchased for you. They get their own delight from watching their gifts being opened, and without saying it, they're hoping you'll like what they brought you. Sometimes they are so eager to have the person open the gift, they'll try and help them get past the wrapping, help them rip off the covering, to get to the gift.

I wonder if that isn't the way God is about His gifts of love for us. Sometimes they come uncovered/unwrapped, and we can see them plainly, but a lot of times they'll come wrapped up in some kind of packaging. Wonder if God, with the same enthusiasm, anticipation and excitement of those little kids at the birthday party, isn't eagerly prompting us, nudging us, saying in various ways, "Open it. Open it. See what's inside. See what I paid for and bought just for you. Go on. Open it. Please." Wonder if sometimes, God doesn't get so eager for us, 'cause we are taking too long or are so slow to discover where they have been placed for us, that God doesn't go on and help us rip off the packaging so we can get to the gift that's been awaiting us. Even so, we must admit that while the gift is the thing we want to get to, unwrapping presents has its own joy and reward.

224

Resist Doubt
There is an enemy that lurks about
Whose weapon of attack is doubt.
He casts his seeds underhandedly
Trying to get them planted before he's found out.
He figures if he can just get you to doubt
He can then take you out.
Remember how in the garden he questioned the two asking what did
God "really say," suggesting slyly it could have been said another way?
With that the seed was planted
And without resistance, it started to sprout.
Watch out!
Don't fall victim to doubt.

Hold fast to hope and tightly to your dreams
Cause doubt is sure that he can weaken you
If he can block them out.
This enemy will try and snatch your dreams,
Crush them beyond memory or recognition before they can get out.
Don't let him!
You are not without a line of attack
If you really want to fight back.
You have armor in your possession that can cause a turnabout
Against whatever schemes the enemy uses to try and undermine your
hope with doubt.
Faith is our Shield and Defender
And Truth, our weapon to resist and fight back.
Faith will keep those darts of doubt and fear from getting through,
And even if they somehow do, it'll keep them from getting to you
If you really believe and live like what you say you do.
If you will raise your Shield of Faith and wield your Sword of Truth
You can resist this enemy, render inoperable his weapons formed
against you
Cause him to step back and retreat
And with God's intervention, eventually defeat.

Kathy Culmer

225

The most tragic victim of unforgiveness is the one who cannot or will not forgive. Unforgiveness is a liar and a thief that comes to steal, kill, and destroy. It lies and tells you that its intended victim is your enemy, the one who offended you; it tells you that they are deserving and that you are justified. But, its real victim, the one it is really trying to get to, is you. It will rob you of your joy, your peace and your possibilities.

The hardening of anything disrupts flow. The hardening of arteries disrupts blood flow. The hardening of attitudes disrupts communication flow. The hardening of hearts disrupts love's flow. The hardening of any one of these is a threat to the flow of life and productivity. Left untreated, they can leave one life-less or leave life less than.

When we choose to remain in unforgiveness, and, yes, it is a choice even though it may be hard and seemingly impossible, and choose not to seek an antidote, The Antidote, It can be like drinking poison unto the soul. What offense, after all, could be greater than those for which a dying Jesus hung on a cross, while pleading forgiveness and offering pardon to those who slay him, even until his final breath?

To pray, "Forgive us our debts as we forgive our debtors" is to pray, forgive us our offenses against You, O God, and against each other the same as we have forgiven those who have offended us. It is a request we make that does not come without its risks, when we ask to be forgiven AS we have forgiven. Perhaps, then, it is more fitting to pray, "Lord, enable us to forgive those who offend us as You have time and time again and once-and-for-all forgiven us."

Kathy Culmer

226

Let the words of my mouth, that which I give life and breath and utterance to, and the meditations of my heart, the yet unspoken words, the seeds of thought that germinate in my heart and become the life of me, be pleasing and acceptable to You, O LORD, my strength and my Redeemer.

Thank You and Amen.

227

Be Your Own Sunshine

Sometimes you have to bring your own sunshine to the day. Shine your shine in your own shiny way. You have to be the one to chase the gloom and the gray away. Sometimes you have to speak words of encouragement to yourself, over and over and over again throughout the day until you believe for yourself what the words say. Sometimes you just have to let the seriousness lay and engage in some serious play. You have to make up your mind that you're going to love yourself for yourself and in spite of yourself because that's the best way to be loved anyway. Sometimes you have to be the best thing that happened to you that day, be intentional about it, and let that be okay.

228

I am glad to know that God loves me no matter what. Some days more than others, I need the fingers of such remembrance to reach out and take hold of me. I need to hear, both with my heart and from its depths, those reassuring words, "I have loved you with an everlasting love," words that carry with them the inherent present-future-perfect promise, "and I always will." I need to feel God's swaddling embrace, with arms strong enough to hold the universe yet tender enough to caress without crushing, arms once outstretched upon a hard wood cross, holding me close enough to feel the Holder's breath covering me and filling me, breathing new life in and out of me. Human love can be fickle, unpredictable, and so conditional. I cannot live without it. But, in addition to, I need a love that just is. No matter what. Some days more than others I need to be reminded of the Greater Love and that I am loved by that Love.

Amen.

229

In everything give thanks.

In everything give thanks for the gifts that come your way, whether you give it in your doing or by the words you say. Let your gifters know they matter and whatever it is they do. Let them know that they matter and that they matter to you.

Thanksgiving is a blessing upon your blesser for something given to or done for you, a blessing that blesses the giver and that blesses you. You never really know the price for what you've received, that somebody had to pay. Expressing thanks allows you to acknowledge some good or good intention that's been spent for you, something that the giver could very well have chosen not to do. Your thankfulness lets them know that what they've done matters, and that they do too.

Kathy Culmer

230

Don't know where they've been all night long, but soon as you get up, the birds are there with their song. Wonder what it is they're trying to say. Is it just a game of play, or a song they sing to greet/make welcome/give thanks for the new day. Whether tweeting or cawing or chirping, .in a voice of their own and in their own way, they seem to say, thank You to the one who made me, for letting me rise and see and sing my song another day. No different than when we, in our own voices and in our own way, give thanks to our Maker when we pray. Thank You for the gift of this day, for the bird's song, and for our own.

Thank You and Amen.

231

Love your enemies. Pray for those who despitefully use you, done wronged you or pissed you off or whom you just generally can't stand or stand the thought of praying for, and if you cannot yet bring yourself to love, to pray, or to pray and mean it, then pray for your own soul until you can. Amen.

232

For those near and dear to us who cannot yet see themselves as You do, open their eyes, O God, that they may see, as You see, just how beautiful You have made them to be. For those who have not yet realized Your love, draw them close that they may feel the warmth of Your embrace, Your touch of grace. For those who have not yet responded to Your call to come, because they didn't hear, or heed, or maybe thought their wilderness or unworthiness too distant a place to come from, Remove the insecurity and doubt that convinced them somehow Your love had left them out. Let them come! For those who think You have forgotten them, or that You could ever, let them know, NEVER! Give them, and us, deep-knowing that we are all (all God's children!), lovely, lovable, and loved!

Thank You and Amen!

233

Be ye holy, not holier than.

The garment of holiness is not one size fits all. Though it bears the same Designer's name, the thread of experience woven together to fit the frame is not the same.

Kathy Culmer

234

Setting Boundaries

I was just fine until I started to think outside the box,
My nice, comfortable box, Where I'd been able to see each line
Stay within and be just fine.
Then, after a while, I started to see
How those lines, that box I'd been thinking in, had hindered me.
Lines, after all, are drawn to define, divide, and confine.
That certainly had been the case for mine.
And, I get it, sometimes within the lines or the box, the box that the lines
create, is where you need to be.
Sometimes lines provide safety, or some necessary boundary,
As long as you don't let them keep you bound, especially don't let your
thoughts get held in captivity.
Once I started looking outside and around, then I started to see
That my box was made up of lines/boundaries that I had myself drawn
for me.

Kathy Culmer

235

In time, about time, on time
Time is steadily moving on
From one moment to the next
It has come and gone.

God, the Creator of time, could have ordered the world to be timeless or could have made time to be seamless, but in God's infinite wisdom, God divided time (moments, days, months, years, decades, lifetimes and times between), and in so doing, God has given us time for rest, reflection, recovery, renewal and restarting, if we would but take the time, so that not only would we have time, but we would have time and time again.

Maybe time is the gift God has given us so that we wouldn't get stuck in the same place, condition, circumstance and stay there too long. After all, day doesn't stay, and night will not last. It's just a matter of time before each has passed. Minute by minute, the last, is a thing of the past. Perhaps time happens to keep us moving along, if we don't stand in its way. Even though we may, we cannot cause time to stop or delay. With or without us, time will keep moving on, anyway. Sometimes too swiftly, we might even say. Moment by moment, day by day, time comes and goes. When? Exactly. No one knows.

And, thus, God created time:
Then God said, "Let there be lights in the dome of the sky, and let them separate the day from the night. Let them be signs to mark the seasons, days, and years."

Time is a gift. Help us, O God, to make good use of your gift.

Thank You and Amen.

Kathy Culmer

236

When I looked up I was already in the middle of the stream, and I started to scream, "I can't swim. Where's the land? It can no longer be seen. Help me! Help me!, Wake me out of this terrible dream."

A voice answered me, "Things are not as they seem. You're not drowning. I won't let you. You're just learning to swim upstream. Catch your breath. Take my hand. Together we'll stroke 'till we reach dry land. You'll build strength and endurance; you'll be better able to stand, to do what you do, what you will, to do what you can. You're exactly where you should be, right on course for your journey, right in line with my plan."

237

The deep is that place where you're in over your head, where you cannot navigate the waters on your own, but must rely on a greater power instead, where you'll have to swim in the water or learn how to tread.

Lord, sometimes You call us into the deep, where untold treasures there You keep, For Your pleasure and Your purpose, You would have us tread farther than we've gone before, leaving behind the familiar, the comfort, and what appeared to be the safety of the shore. It is the way we all at some time must go. Faith's journey requires it so, that our faith may grow and we might come to better know, Your richest blessings there to find when we can leave our doubts and fears behind. Help us, Lord, to answer Your call, let go the land, and take hold of Your hand.

Thank You and Amen!

238

Changing Lanes

Sometimes you have to change lanes on the highway to get to where you need to go. You need to make a turn or the traffic ahead is moving too slow. You assess the situation so you can make your move, then you glide into the next lane real smooth. But sometimes you encounter road construction along the way. UNEVEN LANES AHEAD, the sign will say. So, now you have to reassess your approach to the new lane. Transitions gonna be bumpier than when the road stayed the same. You don't get to turn around in the middle of the highway just 'cause the ride is gonna be bumpy going that way. Sometimes you can't avoid changing lanes if you want to get somewhere, when the lane you've been riding just won't get you there. Some say you need to stay in your lane, but sometimes what you need more is a lane change. If that's what you feel you're being called to do, then know that the road, even though it's not always going to be smooth, is being made ready for you. The bumps, jerks, jolts are reminders of the work that's being done, to make improvements to the road you're on.

Lord, You know us so well. You know the roads we travel, that have been road mapped for us. You know when we need to travel on as we have and when we need lane changes. You prepare us for them and them for us. Help us to hold on when our lanes get bumpy, and we long for smooth roadway. Help us hold to the vision that set us forth on our journey at its start, for the roads we travel and the provision of all we need to travel them.

Thank You and Amen.

239

The Lord is my light
Reveals the hidden
Helps me to see my way
Find my way
Return to the way
In light of His Way.
When light slips away,
Helps me return from the night
Recover my sight
By the light of His light.

The Lord is my light
Light Source of all light.
And my Salvation!
Will stand in for me
Stand up for me
In the way for me
Rescue me
Lie down for me
Pay ransom for me
Be raised
For me.

The Lord is my light
Who gives me my life
Preserves my life
Protects my life
Restores my life
Conquers every enemy
Even death
That threatens my life
Or the life in my life.

The Lord is my light
And my Salvation
Life-giver and Redeemer

Kathy Culmer

Life Source of all Life.
My light
My life
My salvation!
Amen.

240

I pray, O God,
That my faith
Will have roots and wings
That it will have depth and breadth
And height
Keeping me grounded
Yet ever ready for flight
Propelled by Your love
And guided by Your light.

Thank You and Amen.

241

If you sleep in places where the light can get in, It will stir you from your sleep and awaken you. And whether or not you first give in to it or wrestle with it for a while, it will not leave you alone until you answer its call. Lord, help us to remain in places where the light can get to us, where it can move us, shake us and stir us, if need be, until we are fully awake, and cause us to get up, and do, what it calls us to! Your word, O God, is a lamp in the darkness to help us see our way and a guide for us to follow as we live each day. Or could it be that Your Word is the light of Day? Keep us in places, O God where Your light can get to us. Always.

Amen.

242

Sometimes
I'm pretty black and white;
Sometimes I'm kinda gray
Depending on the day
And how I got that way
And whether or not I took the time to pray
And then listened, really listened, and heeded what God had to say.
That can have a lot to do with the color I display
As well as whether I wear just one color
Or an array
In a color-filled bouquet!

Kathy Culmer

243

*"The Lord must wait for [us] to come to Him so he can show [us] his love
and compassion, Blessed are those who wait for His help"*
Is. 30:18

Lord, as You wait for us, to ripen, to repent, to remember, to return, help us in our waiting for You, too. We can't beat You waiting, no matter how much we think we have to do. While we wait for harvest, so do You. While we wait for our blessing to show, You wait for Your seed to grow. We wait to see the manifestation of the thing, while You wait to see Your manifestation in us. Lord, You wait patiently for us. You wait lovingly for us. Help us as we wait on You.

Thank You and Amen.

244

Everything looks so small when looking down from the sky. Not even the mountains look too big or too high. No rivers too deep, nor valleys too low, when you look from on high to the earth down below. Even the clouds that you see don't look bigger than you when the lens of your looking is from an aerial view. Nothing looks unbearable, uncrossable, unclimbable, unfathomable to the eye when looking down from the sky. Amazing how different things can look to you when you look at them from a higher point of view.

245

Help me, O Lord, not to live in regret today, at least not the choke-holding kind anyway. And even if I go there, don't let me stay, just linger long enough to get what I need to move forward, so I don't go back that way. Regret is debt incurred from another day, and not being able to let go is too great a price to pay. Life is far too precious, time too short to let what I did or didn't do take any more life away. So, help me to release my own self from the failings of yesterday (failings in life do not of life a failure make), and let me not be held hostage by regret another day.

Thank You and Amen.

246

Every now and again, Lord, weeds get in my garden, stunting my growth, and causing me doubt, and I need help getting them out. Maybe when I'm not paying attention, or when I get too busy, or too tired, or too anything, before I know, they get in there and start to grow, getting in the way, blocking or distorting my view, choking out life , and keeping the sun/Son light from getting through. When I'm in need of a good weeding, Lord, help me to discern so I can know, what's weed and what's not and what's got to go, so good fruit, God-fruit, can again grow, Your Spirit freely flow, and the handiwork of the Master Vinedresser can show.

Thank You and Amen.

247

Come up higher, You say, O God
into the open air
Though you fear the heights
I will meet you there.

Come out further
from the safety of the shore into the deep
Though you fear the depths
there your safety I will keep.

Come on, You say
away from your familiar place
away from your comfort zone
Though you fear uncertainty
I'll meet you in the unknown.

Come when you discern my calling
leaving what you must behind
Though you fear letting go
All that you ever needed
in My presence you will find.

Come and keep on coming
though you find it hard to trust what you cannot see.
Come with the confidence that when I call
I'm calling you closer to Me.

248

Pray.
All day.
Every day.
It is the only way.

Pray.
Always.
Though it may not keep heartache/hardship away from you
It just may keep you while you're going through.

Pray.
All day.
Any way.
Even when we say amen
The praying does not end
Just to these things attend, Lord,
Until we come to you again.

Pray.
Pray.
Every day.
All day.
In your own way.
While at work or play.
Ask and Pray.
With thanksgiving.

Pray.
For others and the world.
Pray.
In God's presence stay.
Pray.
Without ceasing.
Amen.

Kathy Culmer

249

Your Beloved's Smell

As a teenager, when I went to the movies with my "boyfriend" or a boy I liked, we would snuggle up close while watching the movie. A big part of the excitement of going was that we'd get to be close. In those days, though, the guys, in order to impress their dates I suppose, would wear lots of cologne. In fact, some of them smelled like they had bathed in it. So, after all that snuggling and closeness in the movie theater, you would go home smelling like the one you'd snuggled with. It would be obvious when you left the place, to your parents and anyone else you came near that you had been in someone's close embrace. Close enough to carry their smell/fragrance with you.

How lovely the thought of being so closely held by your beloved that your beloved's fragrance gets all over you to the point that when you go home or out into the world you wear your beloved's fragrance with you.

Certain fragrances, of course, were more popular than others and a lot of guys would wear that same fragrance, but a few, those who I guess didn't want to be like everybody else, would have their own fragrance they wore. They would stand out more, be more identifiable. Then, the people you encountered, familiar with that smell, would say, "I know who you've been with and smile or wink. Yeah, how lovely the thought that you would be held so close in the embrace of your Beloved that those you meet in passing or with whom you linger for a while would be able to tell, and maybe even smell the evidence of your encounter.

250

For the tests You've sent that we've struggled and wondered if we'd ever make it through, sometimes having to have the same test a time or few, 'til we'd learned, done, accomplished, all we needed to, tests that have now become testimonies of You.

For our messes, messiness, and all the messed up stuff that we sometimes do, that when You straighten them and us out become messages of hope for us, and others, too.

For the things that looked impossible, the kinda things in which You specialize, to open our eyes, cause us to realize, nothing's impossible for or with You.

For those times when in our weakness we didn't think we could go on, but learned we were wrong, because it's really in our weakness, those very things that bring us to our knees, where You are best proved, and we are made strong.

For all those things in life we would have avoided if we could, that You dispensed and worked out and meant all along for our good.

Thank You and Amen.

251

All around us storms are raging today, even if we don't yet see them, they are likely on the way. You are the best Anchor, O Lord, to hold onto, the only One Who's been tried and proven to be true. So, please help us, when some storm we come to, not let go and to keep holding on to You, until You have seen us safely through. And, if You Will, help us to help somebody else too, to take cover from, recover from, or simply their own storm to get through.

Thank You and Amen.

252

Daily Bread
Give us this day our daily bread.
Taste and see that the Lord is good.
The Lord your God led in the wilderness,
To know what was in your heart
To know your own appetite.

Give us this day our daily bread.
Taste and see that the Lord is good.
The Lord caused you to hunger, to teach you
You cannot live on bread alone
You cannot survive on oven-baked bread, earthly bread, that will grow
moldy or stale or run out, No matter the taste.

Give us this day our daily bread.
Taste and see that the Lord is good.
Blessed are those who hunger and thirst for,
I am the Bread of Life.

Give us this day our daily bread.
Taste and see that the Lord is good.
Blessed are they who hunger
Taste and see
Blessed are they who hunger
Taste and see
Blessed are they
Who hunger and thirst for Heaven's bread.
I AM the Bread of Life!
For they will be filled.

Give us this day our daily bread.
Taste and see that the Lord is good.
Whoever comes to me will never go hungry.

Give us this day our daily bread.
Taste and see that the Lord is good.

Kathy Culmer

He took bread, gave thanks and broke it, and gave it to them.
Taste and see.
He took bread.
Taste and see.
Gave thanks.
Taste and see.
He broke it.
Taste and see.
And gave it to them.
Taste and see.
Saying, "This is my body."
Taste and see.
Given for you.
Taste and see.
Take.
Eat.
And see.
"This is my body."
Taste and see.
"Broken for you."
Taste and see.
"Take and eat."
Taste and see.
Give us this day our daily bread.
Taste and see that the Lord is good.

God is great and God is good
And we thank You for life-giving food
By Your hand we are led
And by Your love, we are fed
Thank You, Lord for daily bread.

Kathy Culmer

253

Amazing!
I am amazed at
the wideness of the world,
the bigness of the human heart,
the breath-taking beauty of creation
so evidently wrought by the Creator's hand,
the knowledge that I am part of a divine plan
the height and width and depth of God's love
manifest by Grace
overwhelming acts of kindness and generosity
even when,
perhaps especially when,
undeserved or unearned
the grace to make a difference
change a heart
a mind
an outcome
for good
and for God's glory!

Amen.

Kathy Culmer

254

Well-crafted by the Potter's hand
The vessel may, all by itself, in beauty stand.
But when the Potter uses it to pour
Its beauty shows forth all the more.

Kathy Culmer

255

"When you pass through the waters, I will be with you;
and when you pass through the rivers, they will not sweep over you.
When you walk through the fire, you will not be burned, Since you are
precious and honored in my sight, and because I love you."
Is. 43:2;4

When you pass through the waters,
Tranquil or tumultuous, whichever life sends
I will be with you.
To guard, to guide, or to cleanse.
I will not let you drown or be overcome. I will buoy you, teach you to
swim, or make you a stronger swimmer. I will give you the refreshment
that you need. When you are facing rough currents, you will not be
swept away. Hold onto me, and if or when your hands grow too slippery
or you grow too weary, I will hold onto you, come what may!

When you walk through the fire,
You will not be burned. I will be your shield against the flames. I will
fireproof you. Though you may feel the intensity of the heat, for a while,
the flames will not consume you. And if there are scars that remain,
they will be there just as a reminder of what you've made it through.

Daily, Lord, we are going through,
Fire, Flame, or simply the Flow of life,
And as we do, Your promise is that You are going through too.
Help us, O God, to remember the promise, and to remember You.
For all that we go through that reveals more of You
Your power, Your love, Your grace
And that proves Your promises true.

Thank You and Amen.

Kathy Culmer

256

I wonder if God cares about whether we have read the scriptures and how much, and whether we can recite them and how flawlessly, as much as whether we are living them, and how lovingly. I wonder if the measure of our lives will be best assessed by Word count or by Word lived. What if the Word is to feed us not only so that we will be filled but so that others will not have to go hungry? Just wondering.

257

Marinating tenderizes and adds flavor. It requires time and process for marinade to work its way inside and to the core. It is not a hurried thing, although we wish it were sometimes. We may even look for shortcuts. And while whatever it is we're marinating turns out all right, even tastes pretty good, with the shortcut, truth remains, the longer the marinade sets, the more time it is given, the more flavorful, the more tender, and the more digestible can the outcome when it has gone through the waiting. Likewise, the more time we spend marinating, the more we are filled by the marinade.

258

Let our works be a pulpit
From which You preach Your Word
So the message of Your love
Can be seen (in action) and not just heard.
Let our works be as a choir chancel bursting with song
So that its hearers may be consoled or stirred
Some to soothe their souls and some to sing along.
By messages that ring true and clear
And that are to You a sweet, sweet sound in Your ear.
Let our works be acts of worship
Offerings on the altar of thanksgiving
Heartfelt and true
Pleasing and acceptable to You
Always
A joyful sacrifice of praise
A pouring out of heart and soul
Your honor, Your glory and goodness to raise

Amen.

259

When I look up, I can see. When I look up, I can get up. Because I look up, I can!

If all we ever do is look around,
Our vision can get blurred
Our spirits cast down.
What we see can cause us grief and despair
If all we ever do is look around.

Sometimes
We must
look up
Beyond what the eye can see
To move
And to be.
It's by design.
Our anatomy gives us that flexibility.
To extend our visibility
And see greater possibility.

We Must,
from time to time,
look up to see
Look up and out beyond the air
Hope is there.

Perhaps that's at least one reason why
The sun is in the sky,
To catch our eye, to lift our heads and our hopes up high,
To raise our gaze and our praise!

Kathy Culmer

260

While much in life will be credited to you for what you do, even more will be credited to you for what you inspire others to. What you do will one day be all done, but what you inspire others to will keep on doing long after you're gone.

One does not plant a tree so that its beauty for them alone might be displayed, but that the myriads who come afterwards might also enjoy its shade.

261

There are storms brewing. Some are in the forecast, and some are not. Some are already raging while others are quietly moving into someone else's pathway. That is why it is good to know the One who can hold the storm at bay, calm the storm if it comes your way, or safely carry you through.

For those who are currently in the storm, facing a storm, or just being shored up for storms to come…

May God keep you safe through your every storm, raging from within or without and tossing you about, give you wisdom in navigating the storm, grant you peace within the storm, protect you and keep you from direct hits or collateral damage that could be caused by the storm.

May God make every provision needed to move you forward in the aftermath of the storm.

May the blustery winds that once caused such unease become, at God's command, a gentle breeze.

May the waters that once overwhelmed you threatening to overturn your boat and cause it to sink become for you refreshing and thirst-quenching drink.

May the lightning that once pierced the dark sky become a guiding light, and the roaring thunder a lullaby.

May God speak peace to the storms that you face today and those that are on the way.

Amen.

.

262

Some mornings I wake and seem to step right into blessings already waiting on me. Other mornings, the waiting is on me, waiting to get the blessing or to wake up and see. Truth is, every day that You give me to live, You've got blessings set aside (just waiting) for me to get and give.

263

I have come to know, of late, what it means to pray unceasingly, In the morning in the evening and the in-between-time, more and more, if I don't go get them, then the prayers come and get me. Sometimes I even find myself praying the whole day through, with a "Thank You, Jesus" or a "Lord have mercy," (like my mama used to), a "Come quick," a "Help me," or a "Show me what to do," then, there are some times when I just throw my hands in the air, and that becomes my prayer. What matters most to God, I'm sure, is not how it's done or even so much the words we say, but what pleases God most is the homage we pay, the love and trust we show God when we pray.

Kathy Culmer

264

Perhaps the mountain that's in front of you is not there to overwhelm you, but to elevate you, is not there to hinder you, but to teach you to climb or to challenge you to put into practice what you already knew.

The mountain looming large before us, O Lord, is not bigger than You, its terrain not too rugged, its climb not too steep that You can't or won't steady our feet. In its face, please show us what to do and enable us to, go over, around, or make a pathway through. May the journey lift us higher and draw us closer to You.

Amen.

265

Some days you get up, look in the mirror and say, "Sooooo, this is what I got to work with today. All right then, let's work it!"

Some days that's even your morning prayer. That's when you add, "Thank you that I got this to work with today, and that I've got You to work it with me," and you end it with the "All right then, let's work it, which becomes your Amen!"

Kathy Culmer

266

The Gift of Each Day

(It is a gift and not a given.)

When you get a present you open it wide
Dig through the wrapping and trappings to see what they hide
To make sure that you find all of the gift that's inside.
You don't want to miss a thing!

Just as we do not open up our gifts part way,
Nor should we live partly the gift of each day.
Make sure you examine its contents carefully
So you don't miss something that you didn't at first see.

Dig deep if you must or do what you need to
To make sure you don't miss the precious present tucked inside, meant just for you.

This is the day that the Lord has made and gifted to you. How you spend it, in part, is the way you say, "Thank You!"

Kathy Culmer

267

Live Love

Love is not a thing to be suppressed;
It's just a thought until it's expressed.
Love cannot simply be something in our minds
Or be communicated alone in the words we say.
It can start there but it cannot stay.
Love is made manifest when it gets outside of us and in the way
Of our actions and interactions with others
That's how love makes its display.
Love is a thing we cannot keep to ourselves; we must give it and live it
away.
What good does it do us to try to hold onto it or withhold it since it was
never meant to be kept anyway?

Kathy Culmer

268

Room to Pour

Sometimes the Lord takes away so that He can give more. Sometimes what looks like a closing is really an opening or a widening door. God's hand is never empty, but sometimes God's got to have room to pour.

269

If we change our diets—that is, what we consume—and stick to the changes we have made, we just might change our appetites—that is, what we desire to consume. A change in appetite can result in weight loss, a reduction in the excessive and burdensome weight we carry, the elimination of potentially harmful toxins, better health, enhanced appearance, and a more pleasant disposition. Please note that this has nothing at all to do with food.

270

My mother was a master at making biscuits. She could make them look and taste good. The goodness and the prettiness came from the ingredients she used, and the process used to make them. Good bread-making is a lot about the make-up and the work-out of the dough and knowing exactly the right amount of both to put into the process.

Kneading is the working of the ingredients together with your hands until they're mixed up enough to get all the lumpiness and bumpiness out, to get the desired taste and smoothness on top you're looking for. Good cooks know how much kneading is needed before they go on to the shaping and the baking. When the bread is ready, the cook will know, and everybody at the table gets to partake of the cook's delight.

For a God who knows us like this, inside and out, and Who knows the kneading we need and works us through and through to such perfection, and to His delight!

Thank You and Amen.

271

Sometimes the only thing between you and your "healing" is the getting up part. Sometimes to get to your healing, you've just got to get up and move. To get up and walk. To get up off the pallet of worry, fear, self-pity, and pile of excuses you have pieced together and grown comfortably accustomed to and take the next step, even if you have to crawl first to do it.

"Do you want to be made well?" If so, how badly do you want it? Do you want it badly enough to do what it takes to get well?

272

JOY does not always express itself in laughter. It resides so deeply inside that its expression does not always outwardly show, but you know. Within is where it bears its grin. Perhaps that's why the things that give us the greatest joy can bring us to laughter as well as to tears, sometimes all at once. To say that our joy is "unspeakable" does not mean that it has nothing to say, just that it does not always do its saying with words. And when we say that, "The joy I have, the world didn't give it, and the world can't take it away," it is true. The world cannot give you what is not its to give. Oftentimes, the world cannot even recognize your joy or comprehend its source. But, may we, O God, have it, recognize it, and know The Source. Amen.

Kathy Culmer

273

Who would you turn to?

Are you somebody that you could or would turn to if you needed somebody to turn to? Whether in time of need, or sorrow, or judgment, or joy, or just because? If you are not that person you would turn to, what could you do, so that you would turn to you? Maybe you ought to.

274

Stumbling Blocks or Stepping Stones

Why don't you let your stumbling blocks become your stepping stones, the thing to take you higher not crush you down low (or hinder you and turn you around). And if you see and treat them so—those rocks and blocks that once stood in your way just may become the higher ground upon which you stand one day.

Kathy Culmer

275

Wonder who/what I would be
If I were the unedited version of me?
If I would stop trying to be and just let me be?
Would I be pleased with or even recognize that version of me?
Would God?
But God all along could see.
Even the hidden parts of me.

(Before the puzzle was divided God had already decided, from eternity,
who and what my true me, in the image of H/she would be.)

But only if I let go, would I/could I really know.
Or be.
Even so,
Would I want to?
Would I dare to?
Would I want to see the me that lies well-hidden even from me?
Truth be told,
That's what living authentically demands of me.
The only way I can truly be
And ever become the best of me
Or all I was ever meant and made to be.
Then and then only shall my striving cease to be
And my soul set free.

276

Just Sayin'

We can say a whole lot even when we're not saying it. We should therefore and at all times, be mindful of what we're saying, even when we're not saying it with words, so that our saying, in whatever way we say it, is saying what we want it to say. I'm just saying!

277

As I was reflecting on my blessings at the start of a new day, I thought of how I have received so many blessings for which I didn't ask or pray. Though undeserving, God looked past my faults, I don't know how many times, and blessed me anyway, listened to my heart's cry when my words didn't know what to say. All around me and before me, God's love and goodness on display, blessing me any how and any way, even when I cannot real-ize it right away, or fail to be thankful as I often may, still dispensing grace and mercy beyond measure every day, having already fulfilled a debt that in a thousand lifetimes I could never re-pay. I pray that I may live my life in such a way that not only my lips but my life will God's goodness display and my gratitude convey.

Amen.

278

For the chance meetings and the on-purpose accidents, that were never un-intended, but for Your purpose meant, O God. For the holy-hookups and divine appointments we could never schedule on our own, but were already appointed from Heaven's throne. For those things that happen to us that cause us wonder and surprise that were never accidental, but God in disguise. Lord, help us to see You in it, your love, your handiwork, your goodness, and let it accomplish that for which You meant it.

Thank You and Amen.

279

Truth can hold its own. It remains unaffected by whether or not we believe or accept it. It can be distorted, denied, or rejected, yet it remains truth. We, on the other hand, are greatly affected by what we believe and accept as our truth. To recognize truth is the gift of discernment. To accept truth is a matter of choice. To seek truth is an act of wisdom. To know truth and to accept it is to walk in light.

Kathy Culmer

280

Commas and periods are as necessary to life as they are to good writing, for clarity, for understanding and for flow. There are those necessary places where you must take pause before you go on. When you don't take that pause in a sentence, it's called a run-on; in life, well, I guess you could call it the same. Just know that if you keep running-on, you will eventually run out. In both cases, whether reading or living, you will run out of breath. Oh yeah, and in both cases, life and writing, run-ons can cause confusion and disrupt flow, the author's intended message you may miss altogether and never fully know.

Yeah, commas are necessary to give us those necessary pauses, so we can take the breath we need, to move on, getting to know what we need to know, so we can grow as we need to grow. But there goes life getting mixed up with good writing again. We get anxious sometimes with commas, though, fearing they may be periods, and we don't always like endings. But, sometimes you gotta have those periods, too, when the thought is complete and there's no more that the subject of that sentence has to do. So you stop, take a look back, perhaps taking a longer and harder look than the comma requires you to, then move on in a somewhat, though not totally unrelated direction, to live another sentence whose subject is you.

Gosh, the more I explore this thought, the more life, my own, seems to be like a (good) well-structured composition, well punctuated, including some question marks and exclamations, also in the right places, requiring of course, every now and again, here and there a strike-through and some re-writes too, so as to communicate the Author's meaning/message, with clarity, for understanding and with just the right flow—Tellable. Readable. Livable—so that what the Author knows and intended, others can know.

For even this mundane and metaphoric reminder, Lord, that I/we am/are fearfully, intentionally and wonderfully made, and all the care You take in putting together the composition of my life/our lives.

Thank You and Amen!

281

Wisdom is not afraid to say, "I don't know," to let its vulnerability show, to admit it's got room to grow. Wisdom isn't nearly as much about what you know as it is about how you let what you know show.

282

BREATHE life deeply,
But don't hold breath in too long.
Do not inhibit its flow.
'Cause you never know
When it will be all gone.
Savor every morsel, even the bitter to taste.
Don't let a crumb of life you've been given go to waste.
Though life offers many courses, no second helpings are given
That's why you've got to live the life out of the one you are living.
Make the most of the one,
So you'll be filled and satisfied when the one is all done.
And you're left with nothing to do
But take your place among the angels who have kept watch over you.

283

May your hand be upon me, O God, leadinguidingmoldingholdingshapingcaressing me as need be. May your heart beat within me, my life's rhythm and flow, directing my actions and interactions in the way they should go. Let my heart be stirred by the things that stir your heart, moved to do, as are You! Let this mind be in me; Your ways are higher and Your thoughts too. Let this mind be in me—the words of my mouth and the meditations of my heart, let them be pleasing to You. Lead me to love others and myself as You do. Let this mind be in me—more of thee and less of me and more of thee in me. Let this mind be in me which is also in Christ Jesus. In the name of the One who came in flesh to dwell among us and whose death has given us victory over our own.

Amen.

Kathy Culmer

284

Focus directs our footsteps, our pathways and shapes our journey. Focus can even make your way straight on a crooked pathway. What are you looking at with your eyes and your heart? Slaves who wished to escape bondage and dared to run towards freedom kept their eyes fixed on the North Star. No matter the surrounding chaos, no matter the pursuit of the enemy, no matter the barking dogs, no matter the tiredness of the body or weariness of the soul, they kept focus on that bright light in the northern sky. To not do so could result in captivity. While many stars would emit light, only one would lead them to their freedom. What your eyes and your heart are set on, you will follow, knowingly or not, with your heart, your feet, and your affections. Focus can re-direct you when you have lost sight; it can help you navigate the darkness until you can again see the light. Lord, help me to keep so focused on You that even when life gets in the way and is obstructing my view, Your light will still be shining through, and I will keep on following You.

Amen.

285

God is.
In all that you do that you thought could not be done.
In everything that you do and acknowledge that you did not do in your power alone.
In every height that you reach that you could not/would not reach on your own.
In every journey you've taken to destinations-unimagined or long-desired-for
where you could not otherwise have gone.
In every breathtaking moment or divine encounter
that there's just no other way you could have experienced it or known,
or from them grown.
God is.
And is Glorified!

Amen.

286

Some things are too big to be expressed with words. Words are too small to capture it all. Some sound so profound, so resounding it cannot be heard by the human ear; only the heart's ear can hear. Some beauty, so life-giving and breathtaking simultaneously that it renders us weak and unable to speak. Some love, so true that no matter what, it will not let go of you, love you cannot comprehend, that loves you to life, and then to life again. There are times, when our awe and wonder shout our hallelujahs, our voicelessness sings our praise, and a gratitude so deep within us it knows no expression becomes our Amen.

287

Sometimes we need people in our lives to help us hold and hold on to our "big dreams," or maybe even to find them or have the courage to dream them or discover them or recover them or to keep them from becoming night-marish. And yes, while our big dreams are our dreams, having been planted deeply within us by seeds of desire (God's or our own, if not one in the same), in the heart, the soul, our very being, we sometimes need friends and encouragers who can help us carry the weight of our big dreams and help us water them until they have borne fruit, and who will alongside us, savor the sweetness of their fulfillment.

288

The birds are singing this morning. What a welcome sound to wake up to. Cloud-covered sky with no sunshine anywhere in view, still, they do. Do they sing because they know the sun will eventually shine through, or do they just not let the threat of precipitation cloud their view? How about you? Do you sing anyhow, beneath the cloud-covered sky or only when it's blue (the color of the sky and not you)? Or do you only sing when the sun shines through? Or is shining on You? You know, we don't know definitively whether God was saying or singing, "Let there be," back in the beginning, but it just might have been a song that brought what came to be into being. But we do know that what came after that was "all good."

289

Lead us not into temptation. Help us, O Lord, to lay aside, that is, get out of the way of every weight, every snare, every temptation, that entangles us—that threatens to trip us, trap us, try us, trample us; that makes us false promises it cannot deliver, or that in any way hinders us from our blessing or us from being a blessing, so that we may run past or run over or run through; so that we may run on, and on, and on, with grace, the race that is set before us; the race that is ours to run and that none can run for us; the race that is ours to win because of the one who laid the course for us and who is the prize toward which we run, until the victory is won, our race is all run and our work is all done.

Thank You and Amen.

290

You Got a Pass, and You Got a Pass, and We all Got a Pass!

Some years back when I was driving my grandchildren to school, I was stopped by a Constable for speeding. He said I was going 8 miles over the speed limit. Because I was going 8 miles over and not 10, he said he would give me a warning instead of a ticket. I got a pass. Again.

Thank God for pass-es! Hall passes. Event passes. Over passes. By-passes. Back stage passes. Free passes. They let us go or get in or keep going. They give us access to places where we might not otherwise gain entry. They let us get by. Or keep going. To the place of our desire. Without hindrance. And without payment or cost.

Thank you for Your pass-es, O God, that have allowed us passageway, that have allowed us to keep going, keep moving, without hindrance, or cost we cannot pay. Help us to have a forgiving spirit so that we will not hinder or constrict love's flow, to us or through us. For, You have not dealt with us according to our sin. All have fallen short. Yes, ALL have fallen short, no matter the distance.

Help me to remember, Lord, that I got a pass, not just this one time, but more times than I can recall, not the least of which was the one that was paid for on a cross. Clothe me, instead, with a charitable spirit, one that allows me to see the humanity in others, the "me" in others, the God in others.

291

It's like God said, "I'll make them all the same; I'll just make them in
different colors and not tell them, leave them alone and let them figure
out their sameness on their own."

We Used to Play Together
We used to play together every day,
but something happened and it's no longer that way.
We were just fine
Playing color blind,
('til somebody else got in the way with their something to say,
demanding that we only play with our own kind).
Wish we could still just laugh and play,
See the beauty and goodness in one another,
and not be afraid
or let what anybody has to say get in our way.
Who knows?
Maybe we can some day.
We can try anyway.
Can we? Can we try?

Kathy Culmer

292

BREATH-E
Breath.
We think little of it until we can't catch it.
Or it gets taken away momentarily.
Or it hitches a ride on a chilly wind.
Or until it is gone.
It does its work quietly.
In and out.
In and out.
Until it is done.
Life is in the breath.
In and out.
In and out.
Until it is no more.
Breath.
We think little of it.
Yet we cannot live without it.
Eternity.
Just. A breath. Away.
Take time to B-R-E-A-T-H-E
And enjoy every breath.

Kathy Culmer

293

Which is more likely to fill and satisfy? And, why?
Small quantities well-chewed and suited to taste? Or larger quantities consumed in haste? What the body does not utilize, it eliminates as waste. Yet. We cannot estimate alone by taste, because too soon, the taste is gone. Is more always better or less always best? Just wondering.

294

Speak God
There are times,
When we speak God in silence (to quench our soul's thirst),
and we meet God in the quiet;
We testify without sound and our testimony is heard within.
There are times,
When we speak God with words (cause God won't stay silent),
and we meet God in the sound;
We testify with our lips and those within earshot may hear and receive
our testimony.
There are times,
When we speak God out loud with our being (if God is in us, we cannot
help doing so),
and our lives reverberate the sound;
We testify with our living and loving so the world may see loud and
clear,
Believe, and be saved,
Because of what they hear.

Kathy Culmer

295

I don't do much planting. Ok, I don't do any planting. But from the seeds I've seen, they all had a hard outer covering, which means they had to break through something in order to become, and that is in addition to the soil they had to break through as they were growing upward into being.

One way or the other, every living thing is growing
Upward, outward, older, or in some direction.

When a seed grows, does it become something that it was not?
Or does it become more of what it always was, but had not yet come to fully see?
Does it grow into likeness of which has never before been seen or the likeness of the one by whom it was begot?
Yet different as it becomes more or less of self?
Does the seed grow into or out of itself?
By chance?
Or divine design?
Over time.
In time.
On time.
(Did the seed know what it would become before it started to grow or even when it became fully grown? Without knowing when, its beginning or end, how could it possibly have known?)
Does it grow into its own expectation of itself or the will of its creator?
Who makes the seed anyway?
What about us?
When we grow
Do we grow into the unknown or come into our own?
Over time.
In time.
On time.
Does any growing thing grow to become, to become more, or to become so that more can become of or because of how we have grown?

Kathy Culmer

296

"Now to the one who is able to accomplish
infinitely more than we might ask or think"
Eph. 3:20

God has a way.
A way of taking the little or nothing
And making it something more
More than we ever thought it would amount to before.
God has a way.

A way of making the despised and criticized
Into the celebrated and the prized.
God has a way.

A way of turning the wouldn't-give-'em-a-second-thought
Into the highly sought
And the not worth a dime into the worth dying for.

When we can't think, imagine, hope or do a thing more
God has a way.

Thank You and Amen.

Kathy Culmer

297

With all that we as humans can know and can do
There are still some things
We cannot
Nor will we ever be able to
But only in awesome wonder view
The mighty works that God alone can do.
Nobody else, God,
But You!

Amen.

298

MAKE A JOYFUL SOUND TO THE LORD.
Let your days and your ways sing your praise
Without the words.

COME BEFORE HIS PRESENCE WITH YOUR SONG.
With your living and your loving, let your song be sung and heard.

May I make a joyful noise to You, O Lord, with the song of my life—a
composition in the making. May it be a sweet, sweet sound in Your ear,
a welcomed song for You to hear. For every blessed note and measure, I
give You thanks, O God. May it be a joy for me to make and for you to
hear, a pleasure.

Thank You and Amen!

Kathy Culmer

299

Dear God,
Even though You've still got some more molding and shaping to do
before You're through,
I hope each day, more and more You can say,

"Look at my child.
Can't you see?
She's looking more and more like me.
Daily!
That's my child!
Can't you tell?
She sure does wear me well!"

300

I am not a runner and never have been. I am a walker, though, and have been for more years than I can remember. To try and make up for some lost time one morning, I decided to run part of the way. I spotted a place where I thought "It would be nice to run to," but wasn't quite sure I could. I decided to give it a try anyway.

I started out, and sure enough, in no time, I found myself breathless and wanting to quit. Then, I said to myself, "try and make it to that first light post." And I did. "Try making it to the next one." And I made it to that one too. "If I could just make it to the next one," I said, and on and on. Pretty soon, I was looking for and running toward and reaching a new light post for each leg of my run. In fact, I outran my initial goal and made it all the way to the crossing light. Guess what I'm saying is, "Look for your light posts." They are there, even though they may not at first glance be in view, they are there for you, to help you see, find and make your way, and new ways too.

301

You can spend so much time looking for your something else, that you miss your something. So then, you end up feeling that you got nothing, when you could have had everything, if you'd stopped looking long enough to see what you already had.

302

James 1 tells us that if you want to know what the Lord wants you to do, ask. But ask believing, otherwise our minds will be as unsettled as the waves on a tumultuous sea. (With all that rocking back and forth one could easily end up seasick.)

There is an adversary who loves to ride the waves of an unsettled mind to keep us in the blind
Ride on waves of uncertainty and ambiguity that take our breath away make us lightheaded,
and drench us with doubt.
That force us to strain at the oar and distort our distance from shore.
Waves that clip our legs from beneath us so we can no longer stand and blind us so we lose sight of or hope for reaching dry land.
Waves that cause us to swagger and sway
and eventually stray,
if the adversary has a say and gets its way.

Ask and pray. But do so believing. So that you may wait confidently and without the wooziness of being tossed about on a sea of uncertainty while you seek to discern what God has to say.

Amen.

Kathy Culmer

303

You can know without believing, but you cannot believe without knowing. Sometimes your knowing can get in the way of your believing.

Kathy Culmer

304

"To all who received him, he gave power to become children of God"
John 1:12

There are many things that we are given in life or that are made available to us that simply do us no good, because we never fully receive them. There are truths that have not been realized, hope that has not been lived into, relationships that have not materialized, possibilities that have not become, opportunities that have gone unclaimed, faith that has been unable to sustain us, a God who keeps waiting and waiting and waiting for us, because we have not yet received.

When we, or the farmer, or the gardener tosses seed on the ground, it may or may not take root and grow. Even when the seed is planted in the ground, it is not guaranteed to do so. Only when the earth receives the seed and takes hold of it can anything grow. When the earth opens itself up, draws the seed in to itself, wraps itself around the seed holding it close, can something truly wonderful grow. Receiving is not a passive thing. It requires something of us. It requires an openness and a willingness to give up a piece of our own ground so that something else can get in and grow up in us and alongside us.

305

You are our dwelling place, O Lord. In You do we put our trust. Keep your people in safety and in wellness. Shelter us from this present storm and all that may come our way. And when this time of trial has passed, when the storm clouds have rolled away, help us to see the beauty and the brilliance of Your Son, once more shining through, shining upon us and being within us, the light of the world.

Amen.

306

When we are hungry, O Lord, You know what to feed.

Feed us and fix our hunger with the bread that we need. When empty, fill us up, our spirits renew, with the breath of Your Spirit and the power of You. When restless or anxious, with pulses and impulses, racing to get us where we're in no hurry to go, calm us and quiet us, to be still, and know. When we bear bitter fruit, make our bitterness sweet, don't let it take root. Give assurance where we doubt. Where there's fear, cast it out. When we sorrow, let it not hurt too bad or too long; turn it to joy, and give us a new song. When we're bent from some weight, lift us up, make us straight. When there's heart-break, please mend it. From attacks of the enemy, our safety, defend it, where there's sickness, in body, mind or spirit, please end it. Where there's division, give us a way and the desire to work it out. Where we've grown weak in our faith, may our doubt be cast out. Whatever it is that we're going through, help us to bear it, or overcome it, so that it makes the best of us and reflects the best of You.

Thank You and Amen!

307

The Lord is our Provider
We shall not go in lack.
Our Shield and Defender,
Against pestilence, gunfire, hatred, aerial, ground or cyber attack.
The Lord covers us from all sides and always has our back.
Of the sins we confess and the many ways He does bless us
He neither counts nor keeps track.
Where we find ourselves wanting,
He takes up our slack.
Mercy and grace He extends.
His mercy cuts us slack and His grace He will never hold back
His loving care never ends!

Thank You and Amen!

Kathy Culmer

308

Jesus loves us so much that He will perform all manner of miracles to answer our prayers, tend to our needs and give us the desires of our hearts. Jesus loves us so much that He will deny our requests, delay His response, and change our hearts and minds, in order to answer our prayers, attend to our needs and grant us our hearts' desires.

309

Thank You that we got to see another day.
Some, before they could, passed away.
Grace for them and grace for us.

Body and mind still doing their part,
Though maybe not like they used to
Yet some folks can't get one or the other or either of them to do.
Grace for them and grace for us.

Though things may not be exactly as we'd like them to be,
We are not without hope.
While some who do not know God's love
Can scarcely or lack desire to even try to cope.
Grace for them and grace for us.

For folks to love and folks to love us back
While some folks love and kinship lack
Grace for them and grace for us.

Whether with little or plenty,
We are blessed indeed
For there are many who go hungry and suffer from great need.
Blessed are we and blessed to bless.
Grace for them and grace for us.

Thank You and Amen!

310

O Lord, You are not a distant God out there somewhere. You're all around and everywhere. Even when we cannot see or feel Your presence, You are there. Your breath caresses us like air. You dwell within, when we invite and let You in. You did not make us and leave us to go about Your business elsewhere. We are Your business, the crown of all creation, Your greatest affair! As when You first made us, You will forever love us and keep us and shape us with Your loving care. Though at times You are no longer in our view, Your eye is ever upon us, and we are visible to You. When we cannot see your hand, it holds us; or discern Your plan, it guides us; or feel You near, our heart's cry You still hear, whether or not we are aware. "Come," we call, when we despair, and You answer, "I am already there." You are ever near to us, O Lord, never farther away than the distance of a prayer.

Thank You and Amen!

311

Grace
Grace is like air.
We get to breathe it, get life from it, though we did nothing to put it there.
Grace is all around and everywhere, whether we see it or go unaware.
Sometimes it comes as a gift not asked for,
Sometimes as an answer to prayer.
Dispensed, not according to our deservedness, Grace is not at all about fair.
In fact, where we are least deserving, Grace is all the more there.
Grace hung on a cross our lives to spare, taking our places when we deserved to be there.
No deed in our lives will ever compare to the price that was paid—sin's breach to repair.

Kathy Culmer

312

Giants do not walk on their tip toes even when they walk quietly. Tiptoes cannot leave footprints.

Footprints are what we leave behind when we have made an impression on the ground where we have been. While we make our own footprints and are accountable for them, we do no make them for ourselves. We rarely see our own footprints, unless we are looking backwards or retreading pathways already travelled, and do not walk in or follow the ones that we ourselves have made. Instead, we are making them and creating pathways for those who come behind us to follow, for those who will come upon the places where we have already been. It is because of them and how seeing or following or walking in our footprints may shape the making of their own that we should give careful consideration to how and where our footprints may lead them, whether or not they might cause them to stumble or help them to stand, and whether we are creating sinkholes or springboards.

313

At the start of each new day, we are called into the unknown. We arise and enter in not knowing what's in store. Each day greets us with a new and yet unopened door that invites us to come in and explore and calls us to go where we've never gone before. We do not know what to expect or even what we're looking for, or hoping for. But the new day assures us that something awaits, something more!

Unless we live it, open it, venture beyond the door, its contents will never be ours for sure. So, we go. It is a call we must answer; we cannot ignore. That's what both life and faith implore. Get up. Go forward. Life awaits to offer more. Isn't that what faith is for? To accompany you where you haven't been before, though you do not know what's beyond the door.

Faith is not just believing, not just coming to the unopened door. Faith requires us to believe, for sure, but also requires of us more—to move forward without knowing or seeing, though not blindly, for sure, but trusting in the unseen Guarantor, as we move forward and beyond to claim the more held in store.

Kathy Culmer

314

The High Road is often a difficult road to travel, but the view is better, the ride is smoother, and there are fewer stop lights.

315

"He tends his flock like a shepherd.
He gathers the lambs in his arms and carries them close to his heart."
Is. 40:11

When unsteady and unsure from never having walked on their own,
Or too unstable and unable to walk alone,
Or tired and weak from having walked too long,
Or in need of being held by the One to whom they belong.
You carry Your lambs, O Lord.

Those who cannot stand on their own, who cannot walk alone, who are
weary and worn and lost and cannot find their way home. Those who
are afraid and are fearful of the unknown.
You carry, O Lord.

To those who cannot find their feet or heartbeat,
You lend your own.

Always close by, and with a watchful eye, You gather Your lambs in Your
arms and carry them, close to Your heart.

Thank You, O God, for your abiding love that lifts and draws and carries
us, For the watchful eye and loving care of our beloved Shepherd Who
loves us and leads us and lay down His life for us, that we might have
life,
Abundantly.
Eternally.

Amen.

Kathy Culmer

316

The Kingdom of Heaven is like treasure that's right in front of you
though not in plain view.

Treasure that cannot be purchased or earned
That cannot be seen with eyes only, but must by the heart be discerned.
Planted at creation for all humankind
Those seeking with their whole hearts should be so blessed to find.

The Kingdom of Heaven is not just a thing to see
Or of which to merely be aware
But a way to be
And a thing to share!

Kathy Culmer

317

"Your Word is a lamp unto my feet and a light unto my path."
Psalm 119:105

Let Your Word, O God, fall on me as morning dew, to be soaked by my mind and absorbed by my soul.

Let Your Word be as seed planted in my being, over time and in time to take root in me, with roots that run long and deep, to sustain me and keep me firmly planted and grounded in the soil of your truth. Let Your Word produce fruit in me, ripe and abundant, growing up in me, and out of me, other seed to sow, other fruit to grow. Your Word, O God, help me to know its truth, walk in its ways, and reflect its light.

Amen.

Kathy Culmer

318

The wounds are deep
The pain
You feel
Is real.
Cutting deeper by the day
The hurt just won't seem to go away.
You wonder if
The wounds or
The wounded
Will ever heal.

Fear every now and again
Will creep in
Doubt questions if
This nightmare will end.
O, Lord, when?
How much, O Lord, must we bear?
Come.
Quickly.
Save us.
From this time of trouble and despair.

And God answered I am already there.
I haven't gone anywhere.
I have not
Will not
Leave you on your own.
As promised,
I will never
Ever
Leave you alone.

My love will now,
Nor never fail
No matter what, it will prevail.
Whatever and whenever you're going through
I am there beside going through with you,
Beloved,
Working the works that humans alone
For themselves and in themselves
Cannot do
Working all things together for good

And for the good of you.
Amen.

319

Have you ever made a wrong turn that turned out just right?

Ever missed your exit, only to find a new entrance down the street/road/highway?

Have you ever been forced from the left over into the right turn lane?

Have you ever had to swerve to miss hitting or getting hit by something(one) in your blind spot?

Guess you could call it Divine Order for the directionally challenged and the visually impaired!

Lord, thank You for ordering my steps and my tire treads!

Amen!

320

Outside my window there was once a tree.
Its shade covered me.
But because of its branches, I could not see.
Then
A strong wind came along one day
And blew the tree away
Clearing the way for something new
and giving me a fresh wide-open view.
Temporarily.
Then the tree grew.
Who knew?
There were roots in the ground below
Which would allow the tree to once more grow.
(That is the job of roots you know, to hold a thing in place and feed it
what it needs to grow.)
That too is what unforgiveness will do
If you don't get rid of its root
It will grow up again and bear its fruit
Throwing shade and blocking your view.

(P.S. And this you will find to be true
Whether it's about you forgiving someone else
Or you forgiving you.)

Kathy Culmer

321

Help us to live You out loud today, O Lord, not just in the silence of our hearts and thoughts, but out loud, in the actions we take, in our affections for one another, in our regard for You, .in the way we live and love and forgive. Help us to live You in such a way that others can hear and desire to come to You so that they may know You for themselves. We are Your Mouthpiece, O Lord. We are Your Word lived out in the world. May our lives speak well on Your behalf, not causing You shame but exalting You before others.

Thank You and Amen!

322

*"For the Spirit of God has made me,
and the breath of the Almighty gives me life."*
Job 33:4 (NLT)

From time to time, I have experienced shortness of breath. I am extremely grateful for those times when I have full breath, those times when I can take deep breaths and when my airwaves are unobstructed. Breath is essential to life. It was only when God breathed breath into the first human that life entered him. It was the thing that God put in us and left in us to sustain life. And yet, there are moments and experiences and causes that are breath-taking and others that leave us breathless.

I am grateful for breath. Life is in it. It is the shortness of breath, the breath-taking, and the breathless that all added together give us the fullness of breath and life. Thanks to our great and glorious God who gives us breath to live, who graces us with breath-taking moments of awe and wonder in the face of the overwhelming beauty, benevolence, and goodness of God's creation and works, and who revives us from our breathlessness.

Amen.

323

Life is in the breath, the Breath of God. The Lord gives and the Lord takes away. Blessed and Holy is the breath of God!

O, God, who can turn our suffering into celebration, who can make our bitter waters sweet, who can move us from mourning to joy and who alone can raise us to life everlasting, breathe Your breath upon us, fresh breath, Your cleansing, healing, life-giving breath! Let it cover us, fill us, put new life into us. Let Your breath, Your cleansing, healing, life-giving breath flow into us, and let us breathe You in deeply. Let it reach every crack and crevice and corner of our bodies, our being, our world, this whole-wide-world, created by Your Word and designed by Your Will. Let it cure us of our ills and ill-will.

Send forth Your healing balm across this nation and this world and let it heal the fractures and the breaches that have cut deep and wide, viruses and plagues beside, infecting us, fracturing us, dividing us, distancing us, making us sick, even unto death. Restore us to health and wholeness. Resuscitate us with Your love. Remedy us of such unhealthy ways and habits and affections as have caused us our afflictions. Help us to find our heart again, and let it beat in sync with yours.

Life is in the Breath, Your breath, O God. Breathe on us and in us, and let it give us life, even life eternal.

Thank You and Amen.

324

When seas get rough, O Lord,
Help us to hold on.
Help us to remain anchored in You so that we can hold on and not drift
away.

Lord, help us to hold on.
When our hands get slippery
When adversarial winds try and pry our fingers loose.
Help us to hold on.
Through nail-biting and white-knuckled times
When our grips grow loose and fingers are barely touching at the tips.

Help us to hold on.
When holding gets hard and we're just not sure
We can hold any more
Help us to hold as we've never held before
And not let go
Until we reach the shore
And our feet can touch dry land and we can feel
Ourselves safe and secure
In Your hands, O Lord, in Your arms, and in Your love once more.

Amen.

Kathy Culmer

325

Obstacle or Opportunity

The Optimist finds some opportunity in every obstacle that she sees;
The Pessimist sees the obstacles in all her opportunities.
The Optimist will see each stumbling block as a stepping stone.
The Pessimist will see each pebble as a boulder too heavy to carry or
shoulder on her own.

When the Optimist comes to a closed door, she will say,
"Wonder what's behind that door? Let me take a look inside and see."
The Pessimist will look at the same closed door and say,
"There's nothing in this place for me. I can't get in; I don't have a key."
The Optimist sees a roadblock as a mere detour, while the Pessimist
sees it as a dead end for sure.

The Optimist looks toward Heaven and says,
"Ahhh, I can make it; it's just beyond that star!"
The Pessimist says, "I'll never get there; it's just too far."

So much of what we do in life depends on who and what we're looking
at,
Or how we choose to see,
And the places that we get to go,
Depend a lot on where we want to be.

Kathy Culmer

326

Two-handed giving may be done with or without hands. Giving from your hand and giving from your heart are not the same. The hand gives until empty. The heart gives until full.

Kathy Culmer

327

You were,
Destined to be
Love-crafted with possibility
Made
In the image of God
Three in One
And all in Thee
God's likeness to see
And be.

You are
Fearfully
Care-full-y
Wonderfully
Awe-full-ly
Beauty-full-y
(W) Hol-y
Made
And in-the-making
With intentionality!

Still becoming,
As you were in the beginning
Planned and purposed to be
In the mind and heart of God
Being shaped as you are and are to be
By life and a lifetime
Until you have become as one
In this present age
And the age to come.

Kathy Culmer

328

God of the earth and sky and sea,
You cover me.
You walk beside
And go before me.
You stand behind me
And keep watch over me.
You are the solid rock upon which I stand
But even then
And even when
I fall
There You stand
With your powerful hand
To catch me
And set me upright on my feet again.

With eyes and heart
You let me see
You let me know
That you are here with me.
And in the quiet let me hear
Beloved,
Do not doubt or fear.
"Be still" and know
That I AM ever near.

Amen.

Kathy Culmer

329

Some days my heart starts to pray before my lips know what to say. Some days the praise starts to rise before I open my eyes. There's a song in my head though not a word has been said, and the Amen to my prayer is that I get out of bed.

Kathy Culmer

330

Just wondering…

We rejoice in seeing/tasting the fruit of our labor, fruit that is the result of having worked long and hard at a thing, or of achieving some goal or winning some long-fault battle. But I wonder if God doesn't rejoice in our resting, not as in doing nothing, but as in trusting Him/seeking Him/following His lead/obeying Him, as in our resting in Him, while we wait for harvest. I wonder which is sweeter, the fruit of our labor or the fruit of our resting? And to whom?

331

"I pray that God, the source of hope, will fill you completely with joy and peace because you trust in him. Then you will overflow with confident hope through the power of the Holy Spirit."

Romans 15:13

May God fill us with so much light today that we can't hold it all in, that it will shine in us and out from us as we go on our way. May God fill us with so much love as we go about, that we can't keep it to ourselves, we have to let it out. May God give us so much joy that we can't help but do, all that we can so others can have some too. May the peace of God fill us until we overflow, And, may goodness and mercy be our companions wherever we go.

Thank You and Amen.

332

Shine on me, O God, Shine Your light on me
Shine on me, O God, Shine Your glorious light on me!

Where Light abides, darkness cannot go
Let me soak up Your Son-light
Let me bask in the warmth of His glow
That the light of Your love
Will continue to flow
All about me and through me
Wherever I go
That even in darkness Love's light will none the dimmer show
The fire of Your Spirit keeping it aglow!

Amen.

Kathy Culmer

333

For those, whose hearts break today, O Lord we pray, wrap them in Your love. For those whose bodies ache today, wrap them in Your love. For those we love who are lost today, and those who are found, but can't find their way, wrap them in Your love. For those who have some disappointment seen and those who have somehow lost their dream, wrap them in Your love. For those who simply need a touch from You, to remind them that You love them, too, and still do, wrap them in Your love. Hold them close so their hurts can heal and they can feel Your love. O God, our Healer, let your healing power flow through and their strength renew.

Amen.

334

Best Value

There was a time when I thought "Big Gulps," "Super-sized," "All-you-can-eat" buffets, and anything that offered unlimited re-fills were the best values for my money, (To satisfy my taste, so much would go to waste or to my waist). Then, my values changed. Now, I no longer buy, my taste alone to satisfy. The value of the more I once thought I got for less, I came to reassess, when I realized what had cost me less before could in the long term, and often does, cost me more.

335

As uncomfortable as it may be, stripping is sometimes a painful necessity. Furniture is stripped, so that it can receive a new finish; walls and other surfaces are stripped, so they can absorb fresh coats of paint; houses are stripped when former residents move out making way for new residents to move in.

Winter is a time of stripping of the earth in anticipation of spring when new things will grow, The altar in church is stripped as a reminder of the lostness, barrenness, hopelessness in which an unredeemed people once existed, 'til resurrection happened.

Stripping is an act of preparation, a time of making ready. We strip for bathing and for pleasure. God strips us for cleansing and for purpose. It is an uncovering, a removal, a laying aside, to make way for new finishes, fresh coats, new inhabitation, new life.

Yes, sometimes, we must be stripped, uncovered, emptied, so we may be cleansed, get a new finish, made ready for new inhabitation, so that we ourselves may be resurrected. For the loving hands that strip us, that peel away layers of the unwanted, the unnecessary, the unwholesome, the unsightly, hands that lay aside the perishable, to prepare us and make us ready, that then cover us over again, clothing us, finishing us, growing us, meticulously, with the imperishable.

Thank You and Amen!

336

I can sometimes be a mess!
I used to try and hide it
But more and more I go ahead and confess
So perhaps it can bless
When you see I'm not the mess
I once was
Or that my messiness is less
It'll show you God is working
And though He is not finished
He is making some progress.

Kathy Culmer

337

"Who else has held the oceans in his hands?"
Isaiah 40:12

Since time began, O God, we've been kept by Your hands, hands that at creation rounded the earth, hands that have held us since our birth. No battle's been fought, no outcome's been wrought, that's circumvented Your plans and not been in Your hands. Engraved upon them and held closely, never to forget. Not a one of your own have you lost yet. Nor can You. Or will You. Help us to remember, Lord, lest we fret, that You are still holding our lives and our futures, all, and always in Your hands.

Thank You and Amen.

338

You, O God, who shaped the first human from the hardness of the earth, soften the hearts of those whose hearts have been hardened to hate and suffering celebrate. You, O God, who, at Creation, breathed love into your newly created being, bringing love to life, breathe upon us, fresh and new, Your cleansing, healing breath to move us, move within us and flow out from us, restoring life and creating life anew.

You, O God, who, when humanity rejected Your way, went their own way, lost their way, forfeited their way, by Your grace, made a way out of no way, paid the way, the only way, the life-for-a-life-once-and-for-all way, Open our eyes, O God, to clearly see the way. Your way. Find our way. Incline our hearts to choose the way. A better way. Your way. And align our will with Yours to walk upright in the way, into a better day.

Amen.

339

For those, O God, who remain in the storm,
even though the rain didn't last
For those who cannot see beyond the clouds
even when the clouds have already passed
For those who cannot see or find their way back to dry land
because the waters seem non-navigable or too vast
For those who long to feel the safety and assurance of Your love
whether they've known it before or there longing is for once more
May Your love reach them today, rescue them, and return them safely to
the shore.

Thank You and Amen.

340

Dawn,
God's voice calling to awaken us to the new day
His gift and glory to display!
A kiss, a welcome,
God's continuing love and loving presence to convey
Takes us in its embrace to once more say, "Arise, my beloved, I have
gifted you a new day!
(Dawn not only calls us to; it calls us to do,
"Arise. Shine. For your light has come!)
And I am here to guide you and be with you,
Come what may,
Every step of the way."
For the dawn and the dawning
The light that it brings
And the day that it becomes.

Thank You and Amen!

Kathy Culmer

341

"Do to others as you would have them do to you."
Luke 6:31

The way people treat you says more about them than about you. It speaks their truth more truthfully than words could ever do.

The way you treat others says volumes about you too. It speaks your truth better than words could ever do. It's up to you to make sure that the way you treat others says about you what you want it to, and tells the truth about you that you want to be true.

342

Sometimes love means running at a slower pace, so your loved one can catch up and run along beside. Sometimes love means running ahead of your beloved and lovingly encouraging him or her, letting them know they can run faster or that it's okay if they can't when they've tried. Sometimes love may even mean letting your loved one find his or her own stride while you cheer and look on with loving pride. Whatever the case, love means putting yourself aside so you can best decide. Whatever the pace, love is above all about who you want with you in the race, to the finish, by your side.

Kathy Culmer

345

Everybody's grace doesn't look the same.
Grace doesn't manifest itself the same way,
though it is dispensed to each of us
as a gift for which we do not have to pay.
Since we don't know the cost
And its value we cannot weigh
(We couldn't pay it fully anyway)
Then we can hardly say
That mine or yours is more or less.
Not truthfully anyway.
Just thankfully receive it as it is given
And be willing, where and whenever we can,
to give some away.

Kathy Culmer

346

Side glances only give you a partial view; they can't possibly tell the full story of what's in front of you; nor can you count them as proof that what you think you see is really true. That's the risk you run when you compare yourself to others without knowing what they've been through. You can if you want to, but it'll just keep you second guessing yourself and what you do, or have you thinking either too highly or lowly of other folks when you spend your time comparing yourself to others or them to you.

347

Grief

Is the last thing of our loved one's earthly presence that we get to hold onto. It is our heart's cry and love-filled good-bye to our beloved when they die, a parting embrace, a slow release into their resting/waiting place. It is a strange combination of mourning and celebration, of longing and letting go, though never fully. For some, not wanting to let go, we hold on too long or too tightly. But grief held onto for too long or too tightly can eventually become a thief, robbing us of its eventual and intended relief.

348

Mother
Though she rarely had a dime to spare,
Never did I doubt her care
Nor would I dare
'Cause all the time and everywhere
I was well aware
That she covered me with prayer
To protect me and to prepare
me for the world out there
Loving prayer that I could feel,
and do still!
Who knows, maybe that's her legacy I'm living when I share
My thoughts of God and of you in a prayer.

349

Lord, I thank You
That when I come to the edge of myself, You keep me from falling off
That when I am beside myself, You are there too
That when I bend beneath whatever weight, You won't let me break
That You make me and my way straight again
That when I have lost sight of me, I am still recognizable to You
That You've never let me wander beyond the reach of Your hand
Or get so far gone I can't find my way back again.

For all the times, O God, You have kept me or kept me from.
That You keep me still, and You always will.

Thank You and Amen.

Kathy Culmer

350

"O Lord, you alone are my hope."
PS. 71:5

Hope did not wait for its heart's desire to come and get it.
Instead, Hope got up and got going until it had met it.

That it didn't go sooner or faster or try harder, Hope refused to regret it.
Carrying such weight can hinder hope, and Hope refused to let it.

Hope says I can, and I will, even though it's uphill.
Though tempted, at times, Hope maintains its resolve, refusing to give in
to its tempters and let them upset it.

My hope is in the One from whom my help comes. My help comes
from the Lord.

Thank You and Amen.

351

Writing, and being written, daily, and not just with words!

Be the publisher of my day, O Lord, the author of my thoughts, the illustrator of my way. According to your plan, your purpose and design, help me daily to live my story in your story and let them always align. Be at my center, O God, so that my pages give You glory. Be my cover and my spine. With your love bind your story to mine, eternally, my Editor-in-Chief divine!

Thank You and Amen!

352

Hunger (Some thoughts to feed upon)

By design, we do not take in all the nutrients we need all at once or with one meal. We eat in increments. Even though we might choose to eat one meal a day, it cannot provide us all the nutrients we will need for the day or fill our hunger for its entirety. We, by design, consume the nutrients and the calories we need to sustain life a bit at a time. We are made to get hungry over and over, must be fed and filled repeatedly to satisfy hunger, meet our needs, maintain and sustain life. To try and take in all we need at once would create an imbalance, leaving us too hungry at some times and too full at others. This could result in discomfort and interfere with our ability to perform at an optimum. We simply don't have the capacity to take in all of what we need at once. Just as our bodies must be fed to be sustained and satisfied, so must our spirits be fed.

Like our bodies, neither are our spirits able to consume all they will ever need all at once, but must be fed in increments, must experience periods of hunger and cravings and changing appetites. Nor can we take in all of God at once. God is too much for our plates and our digestion to hold, comprehend or consume all-at-once. To sustain our bodies and souls, to provide them all they need and require, we must keep on hungering, though to different degrees, and keep on being fed, perhaps with different portions, whether with food or with God, daily and throughout the day, for the journey of a lifetime!

Give us, Lord, our daily bread.

Thank you and Amen.

353

The mirror exposes stuff. Sometimes we avoid looking at it or looking at it directly because we don't want it to show us what we don't want to see. It does not hide or distort. It simply shows what is. Whether we like it or not. Whether we want to see it or not. It forces us out of denial into knowing. It shows us our beauty marks, yes, but it also exposes our blemishes. Some will ignore them. Some will deny them. Some will squeeze them. Some will resign themselves to having them there or leave them alone in hopes that they will go away. Others will seek remedies to clear up the blemishes. Blemishes are always an indication of or the result of activity that is taking place beneath the surface. The mirror's job, however, is not to fix our flaws, but to show them to us so we can know. So we can decide. Knowing. So we can do what needs to be done. So they and we can heal.

354

If I am not careful, I can hold on so long to negativity
It can flip the grip and get a grip on me
Make me blind so I can no longer see
Any kind of positivity.
It can leave me in such a state of misery
Where constantly, I demand, deny and disagree.
That's not the me I want to be.
Lord, please don't let it get the best of me.
Release me from captivity
Cleanse my thoughts and set my vision free
'Cause the way I see, has everything to do with the me I'll be.

Kathy Culmer

355

I wonder, If God didn't give us sleep, not only so we could rest, but so we could wake up. So that new days could keep breaking and we could keep waking. So that we would have the chance to open our eyes (or have them opened for us) again and again, and see what we haven't seen before or to see it anew. If we are willing and want to. Rise. Shine. For your new day has come!

356

When our loved ones pass from sight, they do not remain with us as distant memories, but in time become as close to us as thought and breath. They settle into us, seeping into the fabric of our being, their threads with ours intertwined to shape the shapes and patterns of our design. No longer external, love loves from within, .a part of us, and life itself, eternal.

Kathy Culmer

357

Every time they're widening the highway or doing road repairs, they always have to shut down some of the lanes while they're working on the road. As a traveler, you're inconvenienced. You get delayed. You may even have to take an alternate route while the work is being done. Sometimes that's the way it is; you have to experience some bumps, delays, and re-routing, or even go out of your way, to get to your destination when you try to make improvements to the road you're traveling.

358

"The Lord helps the fallen and lifts those bent beneath their loads."
Ps. 145:14

Falling is inevitable.
Trip or stumble we may
Over obstacles we encounter
Along life's pathway.
For certain there will be times when
Our knees will grow weak
And our legs will give way
Whatever the cause,
We will stumble and fall.

But God.

We get up.
We do not fall to stay fallen, no matter how often or the cause of the
fall. Even though our knees and our egos may get bruised when we hit
the ground and our gait may be altered when we get up, we get up.
Sometimes we fall down so we can know how to get up or know that
we can get up. Sometimes it is because the ground on which we were
walking was not solid ground and just gave way, and the fall was to
encourage us to go another way. Sometimes we fall down so we can
look up and see, and know or know better, the One who can raise us to
our feet again.

A bent knee or a prostrate fall is sometimes what is needed most to
help us stand tall. Amen.

Kathy Culmer

359

Morning Walk

Wind-kissed by chilly lips
Embraced by the cool breeze
Whipping through the trees
Trees now nearly bare
Having disrobed their leafy outerwear
Once more to wear
When spring returns.
Summer's gone
Though remnants linger here and there.
Nevertheless
I am blessed
And refreshed
By the morning air
Oh, how I have missed my morning walks and talks in open air!
Seasons will change
It is their nature to do so
But God's love remains
This I know.

Kathy Culmer

360

One of the greatest gifts you can give ANYBODY is to make them feel that they matter; an even greater gift is to let them.

Kathy Culmer

361

Outside the Lines

I used to always color within the lines or think that I had messed up when I didn't. Then, I realized, some people color outside the lines because they don't know how to color within them. Some may color outside the lines because they refuse to let lines confine them or define them. And others may color outside the lines because they like the picture they get when they dare to do so. Lines are fine, but they were drawn by someone who once saw things only the way they look within the lines. Lines do not always, however, mean there is no other way to see the picture or that there is only one way to color it.

Kathy Culmer

362

"Evening passed, and morning came."
Gen. 1:19

I am grateful for the sunrise,
When day is overtaking the night
And bringing back the morning light.
Blessed are they who behold dawn's face, who receive and return her warm embrace.
For they shall be energized and renewed by morning's grace!

I am grateful for the sunrise,
For its waking and its staying power
For the assurances it brings to each new day,
I am still with you; I have not gone away.

Sunrise is the mark of something new and simultaneously a reminder of the eternal too. Beginnings and endings, closing out the old and giving rise to the new
If that is what it needs to do,
But for the ongoing, our strength to renew.

Steadfast, immovable, glorious in its appearing (its coming and going)
That which is rising but does not itself move. It is we who do.
But only in and out of view.

Thanks be to God! Amen!

Kathy Culmer

363

Each day is spent
A purchase made
How you spend it
Is what you paid
No refunds, exchanges, change back
Or even trade.
So make sure you've counted the cost
And your options you've weighed
Before each purchase is made
To make sure that when the spending is done
You don't come up short and haven't overpaid.

Kathy Culmer

364

Being grown
Doesn't mean not having to listen to anybody any more,
But knowing whose voice to listen to and whose to ignore.
Being grown
Doesn't just mean doing everything
You want to
But is when "just cause you want to"
Isn't the only thing guiding what you do.
Being grown
Doesn't mean there's no more growing for you
But realizing that no matter the age you live to
You are never fully grown
And that there's always some more
Living
Learning
Loving
Growing
You can do.

Kathy Culmer

365

The Lord is my Shepherd,
My Guardian and my Guide.
The Lord is my Protector
In God's shelter I'll abide.
Covered by a love that won't quit and can't be denied,
For the sake of its beloved was once crucified.
Everything I need—
Everything!
The Lord will provide
And my heart's desire beside.
Each day multiplied!

Thank You and Amen.

Kathy Culmer

366

Lick the Platter Clean

When I was a girl, and I had eaten something that was especially good to me, maybe a bowl of ice cream or a piece of apple pie, I wanted to make sure I got every bit of taste out of it that I could. So when I was done with its contents, I would lift the bowl or plate to my mouth and lick it clean. (Not good manners, I know, yeah, yeah, yeah.)

That meant that whatever it was I had eaten was so good that I wasn't willing to let a drop of it get away or go to waste. I treated it as though I would never get another taste of ice cream or apple or lemon meringue pie, or whatever it was, again!

Eat it up. Eat it all. Savor it. Enjoy it. 'Til the last drop. Then, 'til the platter's clean. Terms we typically associate with a good meal, food for our bodies, food that has been prepared for our nourishment and enjoyment by loving hands. While it was not a display of good manners, it was a high compliment to the cook when you licked it clean.

What if we looked at life the same way, what about a new day that's been lovingly, carefully, and joyfully given? What if we approached each new day with the determination to get every good thing possible out of it? What if we lived it as if it were that cherished and delectable dish that we simply can't stop going at it until we've gotten every morsel of good out of it that we can cherishing each bite of it, each chew of it as though we would never be granted another? Eat it up. Eat it all. Savor it. Enjoy it. 'Til the last drop. Then, 'til the platter's clean. It is the highest compliment to our Creator when we "lick it clean."

Let us, therefore, eat heartily, taking care not to miss a crumb of each day, even though some items on the menu might not be to our taste. The gift is in being given the day—one like no other, one you'll never see or taste again, one that some were not given. Partake of it as such. Live it to the full. Get every morsel you can out of it. Enjoy it thoroughly, and then, if you dare, lick the platter clean.

Kathy Culmer

This is the day the Lord has made, the life that's been given, let us rejoice and be glad in it!

Made in the USA
Columbia, SC
16 December 2022

74068313R00211